Runaway Amish Girl:

The Great Escape

By
Emma Gingerich

Published 2015 by
Progressive Rising Phoenix Press, LLC
www.progressiverisingphoenix.com

ISBN-13: 978-1-940834-07-8

Printed in the U.S.A.

Cover and Author Photos by Zach Weber Photography

Original Book design by eBook76.com

Case Edition Book and Cover design by William Speir
Visit: http://www.williamspeir.com

Acknowledgements

I would like to thank first and foremost Mitch Haynes, the mastermind behind Lexicon Writers conference. He encouraged me to follow my publishing dreams and not give up. I gratefully appreciate and thank David Hughes, for his editing services, he did an amazing job. I want to thank Author Amanda Thrasher and Author Jannifer Powelson, owners of Progressive Rising Phoenix Press, for their hard work in getting the book to print. They truly have been a blessing to work with. And thank you to Zach Weber and his photography business for working with me on the photos for the cover. He knows his art!

On a more personal level, I want to thank Bill and Laura Jo Turnipseed, and Scott and Tara Williams for their continued support and for asking me a million questions. Answering questions inspired me to write a book so I don't have to answer anymore!

Dedication

To Dad and Mom, Brothers & Sisters,

If you should ever read this book, I hope you can finally understand why I left home. Sometimes you just have to follow your heart and let God be in control of your life even though it doesn't make sense. Trust in yourself and live the life that's meant for you. Although we are in two different worlds, my thoughts and love are with you daily.

This whole book is about the Swartzentruber Amish community.

Chapter 1:

Ask for Forgiveness not Permission

I am deliberate and afraid of nothing.

~Audre Lorde~

Rules, rules, rules! You cannot have a phone in your house. You cannot have electricity. Your dress has to be a certain length. You cannot take sightseeing vacations. The windows in your house cannot be too big. The list goes on and on. I thought about these rules as I cruised down highway 499 in my maroon 2001 Dodge pickup truck, air conditioner and radio both cranked up. I was on my way to Texas State Technical College in Harlingen where, at 19 years old, I had just begun my journey in educating myself. I had no clue what I was doing, but finally escaping from so many pointless rules filled me with a sense of relief so deep no one else could ever fully understand—unless, of course, that person grew up Amish.

As the tires hummed and the truck headed south, I thought about the handwritten letter I had just received from Sarah and Amanda, my younger sisters back home. Out of fourteen children, I was the oldest of the girls, and I had one older brother—Jacob. I smiled as I reminisced about my two favorite little pals. Reading their letter brought back memories of the crazy things we used to do together. Well, as crazy as three Amish girls could get. Sarah and Amanda were only a year apart and sometimes folks mistook them for twins because they were the same size, but they did not look the same. Sarah was fourteen, with blonde hair and blue eyes; she looked just like Mem, except for the fact that Mem had dark hair. Amanda was thirteen and looked and acted a lot like me. She had dark brown hair, green eyes, and was more serious about life, like Datt. They could wear each other's clothes and often did things together as best friends. In fact, their friendship was so close it would not surprise me if they wound up getting married on the same day. After all, the Amish do have double weddings sometimes.

As alike in age and appearance as the two girls were, their personalities were very different. Sarah was full of humor and jokes, as if she did not have a care in the world. I could always read her mind and could tell when she had something up her sleeve. She would have an ornery look on her face and become a little overly talkative. Where Sarah was mischievous and easygoing, Amanda was more serious and could easily get angry when someone got under her skin. When she was in a good mood, however, she could light up a room with her witty remarks. I missed them very much, but unfortunately, I was now the outcast of the family, a dove whose wings could never quite be clipped. I now knew I probably would never have the same relationship with them as I did before I flew the coop. The thought choked me up.

As the Dodge's wheels hummed toward my future, I continued driving down the path of my memory; I could see their mischievous, giggly faces as if it was just yesterday when we had made fools of ourselves. As confined by rules as my Amish life was, it seemed almost anything could remind me of my past: the smell of a feedlot would bring back memories of my datt's cattle and sheep barn that eventually went to nothing. The whisper of wind through the leaves reminded me of the nights I would sit in bed, leaning against the wall, and wonder why my life had become so frustrating. On that road to college, the pickup brought to mind when I was almost seventeen and Sarah, Amanda, and I came as close to becoming criminals as we could. In a heartbeat, the memory of the unexpected night of walking home barefoot when the truck we had stolen broke down tumbled into my head. At the time, I did not think about the morality of what we had planned to do. I just craved a taste of freedom and excitement.

As that Saturday evening approached, my cousin Eli and I had the plot to steal the old pickup truck well underway. Eli was the same age as me and was also one of our neighbors. His mem was my datt's sister.

We hatched our plot one night while I babysat at Eli's house; his parents had taken a trip out of town to visit family and friends, and we could not pass up the opportunity. The Byler's did not leave town often, so it was the perfect time to get into a little mischief. Since it was Saturday night, Sarah and Amanda decided to spend the night with me and help babysit Eli's three little brothers and his baby sister. My sisters had no idea what we planned to do, and I could not wait to tell them. We had to wait, though, for the whole neighborhood to settle down for the night before we could spring the plan into action, so I took the opportunity to fill my sisters in on our agenda.

"Hey," I whispered to Sarah and Amanda, making sure none of the little kids overheard us, "guess what we will be doing tonight?"

"There is no telling what have you planned," they said in unison.

"What will we be doing?" Amanda asked.

Their faces glowed with excitement as I told them about the old pickup truck I saw on top of the hill as I drove home from town earlier that day. As soon as I saw it, I knew that if the keys were in it, we would take it for a ride. Before Sarah and Amanda arrived, I had already filled Eli in on my intention to sneak up the hill to "borrow" the truck and go for a cruise. At first he laughed at me, but he soon realized I was serious.

"You don't know how to drive," Sarah piped up, her round blue eyes widening with fright.

"I know, but surely it can't be that hard." I tried to sound confident. "I will drive in the plowed field first, to practice."

"I think one of the boys should go with us," Amanda added.

"Okay, I will ask one of them to go with us, just to be on the safe side."

We waited for Eli's brothers and sister to go to bed and fall asleep; we could not take the chance of one of them snitching. They finally fell asleep by ten o'clock.

Two other boys in the neighborhood, Levi and Noah, came over that evening to spend the night too. The boys filched a four-wheeler out of a neighbor's garage without permission. The neighbor was only home during deer hunting season, so they thought there was no way anyone would ever know. The boys headed up the road to where the old farmer had left his truck while we waited on the side of the road close to a bridge. No water flowed under the bridge—it had gone dry over the summer—but howling noises erupted from the dark woods nearby. Amanda shuddered and glanced around. Sarah stood coolly, a smirk drawn on her face. I was too excited to be nervous or scared. I felt like nothing could go wrong when my sisters hung out with me.

We were about a quarter of a mile from Eli's house. It did not seem that far away, but if one of the kids woke up, there was no way to hear the cry.

Luckily, the keys were in the truck, as if it sat waiting for us to take it out for a cruise. The boys promised I could drive after they got it started. Eli and Noah gunned the four-wheeler further up the dirt road to a dead end to play in the mud.

Levi climbed into the pickup and drove it back to where my sisters and I waited by the bridge. The headlights shone brightly as the truck rattled down the hill. As soon as the pickup stopped, I jumped in first, with my sisters tagging behind. All four of us squeezed into the front seat, eagerly anticipating a great evening of unforgettable fun and excitement. This was definitely something different from the cooped-up life we lived at home week after week.

Levi drove north toward my parents' farm, and nervousness crept over us as we approached it. *What if this horrible old truck stops right in front of the house?* I thought. The engine made a loud sputtering noise that hurt my eardrums. I was sure Datt could hear it from his bedroom. I pictured him looking out the window and seeing four guilty Amish teenagers sitting in an old stolen farm truck, and I was sure he would fly off the handle and never forgive us for such mischievous behavior. I could not even begin to imagine what our punishment would be. In some Amish communities, *rumspringa,* or "running around," was a time when teenagers could do anything they wanted. They could go to clubs, dance, drink alcohol, and change into modern clothes for a wild night out on the town. Some kids would even buy a car to use on the weekends, but would keep it hidden. Parents were expected to look the other way and hope their children decided to give up their worldly desires and join the church when the time came. Unfortunately, my community did not practice *rumspringa,* so we would be in a heap of trouble if my parents found out what we did.

If we got caught with the truck, everyone in the community would know. I shuddered at the thought of my friends staring at me and whispering behind my back the next time I went to church. But then again, I was getting used to girls talking about me. *Why should I even care what they think*? I wondered. All my friends seemed to be so well-behaved it was awkward and boring to hang out with them. I did not fit in no matter how hard I tried. I used to tell myself, "Tomorrow I will start behaving like a young lady just like I am supposed to do." However, tomorrow never came; I continued doing what I did best, and that was pushing against the rules.

Levi pressed on the gas pedal and the sudden acceleration yanked me from my thoughts of getting caught. As we approached my parents' farm, my sisters and I held our breath. Whew! We whizzed past the house with no problem. Now we could relax and have some fun. The radio blared... My sisters laughed... No annoying bonnets clung to our heads... no shoes smothered our feet. All my sisters and I needed was a pair of jeans and a tee shirt so we could ditch our long dresses for a bit. I knew that would not happen tonight, but for the moment we enjoyed an unforgettable adventure. My dream to drive a vehicle was finally becoming a reality. Or so I thought.

We drove to a small town about seven miles away and stopped to buy some gasoline for the truck. We paid with cash, and the cashier stood slack-jawed when he saw what we were doing. He probably wondered how Amish kids managed to get away with a vehicle.

"If he is smart he will realize we stole this," I told Sarah and Amanda.

As we confidently walked out the door, we smiled and waved at him. He waved back and a little smile cracked his face. Great! Smiling was a good sign!

"I hope he doesn't call the cops," Sarah laughed nervously.

"Nah, we will soon be out of sight and forgotten," Levi assured her.

We started back home by a different route. My sisters and I looked forward to taking a turn driving as soon as we hit the gravel road. For a long time I had secretly contemplated leaving the Amish, and tonight was the perfect opportunity to start learning how to drive. For the past several months I had been peeking into parked cars every chance I got to figure out how they worked. I especially wanted to learn which pedal was for the gas and which was for the brake. It puzzled me that people did not get them confused.

"Levi, can you pull over and let me drive now?" I yelled over the noise of the radio and the roar of the wind howling through the open windows. I could not wait any longer to get my hands on the steering wheel.

"Are you sure? I think you should wait until we are on the gravel road. It is not as easy as it looks."

Sarah and Amanda yelled, "Let us out before she starts driving!"

"What is the matter with you girls?" I turned and looked at them; both returned my gaze, faces serious. "You are supposed to be supporting me," I reminded them. "It was my idea to take the truck and you had a choice whether or not to come along."

Sarah leaned close to my ear and yelled, "You are going to scare us!"

"Owww, you are making me deaf yelling like that in my ear!"

Less than ten minutes later my anticipation of driving was crushed, and we ended up walking home. Our trashy stolen truck quit running while bouncing down Main Street right in the middle of another small town. We had just turned left at a stop sign when the engine popped loudly and the truck drifted to a complete halt. It scared the dickens out of all of us!

Levi jumped out and opened the hood. Thick black smoke poured from the engine. Talk about frightened sisters! Sarah and Amanda both resembled stiff white ghosts haunting an abandoned graveyard. I am sure I probably looked the same or even worse. It was just like one of those many dreams I had where I was scared and tried to move but could not. Now the horrifying dreams had become reality. The town was very quiet except for dogs barking and the occasional vehicle driving by.

I knew we deserved to be punished for stealing the truck, but did it really have to happen right here and now? If we made it out alive, we could end up in jail, which was an unimaginable thought. I had never heard of an Amish person being arrested, but it could have been possible since many things in the Amish community are kept secret.

"If we get arrested," Sarah said, "why don't we live somewhere else after we get out of jail?" She suggested running away and renting a house and live like the "English" do. We used the term "English" for anyone who is not Amish.

Sarah did not know at the time I had already planned to leave. Now I wondered how she would react if I told her I was seriously thinking about running away. *Would she want to go with me?* I thought. We had talked about escaping many times but it was always just in fun, and I was not ready to let her know how serious I was.

Amanda sat in the cab, too scared to say anything. She stared at the smoke, hypnotized.

At that moment, we had only one choice: get out of the truck and run! I yanked Amanda's arm to get her moving. The truck sat stranded in the middle of the street. We could not roll it off the road because it sloped uphill. We could not back it downhill either because the truck had broken down right in front of an intersection. So we left it sitting in the road, hoping no one would run into it when they turned at the stop sign.

Unfortunately, we were four miles from Eli's house, and one of those miles consisted of a gravel road, which we now had to run barefoot on since we had left our shoes at home. We ran for a while, then slowed to a jog. Every time a vehicle approached from behind, we slowed and walked normally to minimize suspicion. After three miles on the paved road, we arrived at the gravel road. Thank goodness running around outside barefoot for years had hardened the soles of our feet like shoe leather, so we hardly noticed. We made it safely back to Eli's house, and I breathed a sigh of relief when I found all the little children still sound asleep.

After Eli and Noah returned with the four-wheeler and listened to our story, they rode back to town to see if the truck was still there. As they approached the intersection, they saw cop cars surrounding the truck, so they turned around and raced back home as fast as possible. We stayed up most of the night worrying the police would come pounding on the door and arrest us. We finally concluded they would not be able to prove we did it because we did not have Social Security numbers. I do not know why we arrived at such a lame conclusion, but for the moment the thought comforted us.

I later learned the truck owner lived about two blocks from where it had broken down. I wondered what he thought about his pickup being abandoned in the middle of the town he lived in and four miles from where he had left it. At least he got some free gasoline out of the deal! I do not think anyone would have suspected Amish kids were the culprits. The outside world often perceives the Amish as innocent and would do no wrong. And it was even more unusual for girls to do something this extreme, as they were always at home with no chance to get out.

§

The endless flatness and tropical palm trees of South Texas whooshed by as I approached the college. After I arrived at the school and sat in the classroom, I wondered if my head was going to crack from all the information I now had to retain. When I read the letter from Sarah and Amanda, I wished they were here with me, but not so we could steal any more trucks. I wanted them here so we could take this journey together. I had left the Amish with a very poor eighth-grade education and I did not speak much English, only German. Now I suddenly found myself attending college full time less than two years after I had left. Talk about culture shock! But instead of letting my childhood memories go, they are now more vivid than ever with each step I take to better myself. However, I am constantly reminded of my sisters who are still back home with a future determined only by a repressive tradition stretching out before them.

Chapter 2:

Babies Come from Airplanes

*Nothing ever goes away until it teaches
us what we need to know.*

~Pema Chodron~

If only people could see where I came from, they would
understand how petrified I was to leave the Amish, the only
life I ever knew, and transition into "English" life. The
culture shock was bigger than I had imagined. There are
many different groups of Amish; my family is from the
"*Swartzentruber Amish*," which is a group of the least
modern and uneducated Amish people on the planet. They
are sometimes referred to as the *knuddle-rollas* (dirt-
rollers). They got the nickname because they take a bath
only on Saturday nights, and sometimes not even that often.

Even though Amish have a problem with hygiene, their
clothing style is very meticulous and has to be followed to
the point. I always thought women were required to cover
up way more than necessary, but since I liked to push
against the rules, it probably seemed much worse to me.

Women are not allowed to cut their hair, but are
required to wear it under a bonnet that covers the ears. They
have to fix their hair into a bun and wear a black or white

cap (depending on the age) completely covering every strand. The white cap is worn after a girl turns fifteen; before that age they wear a black cap during the week at home. For weddings and funerals, every girl and woman wears a white cap. For regular church services, only the married women wear a white cap and the girls wear a black one. It gets a little confusing to understand all the different ways to wear a cap, but it is a major essential for Amish women, who are required to wear a cap at all times, except while sleeping.

There is only one style of wearing hair among Amish women, and that bears very little improvement from generations ago. Their hair is parted exactly in the middle and combed smoothly down toward the back, where a dark-colored cloth band is started and carried around on each side, then their hair is gathered into a bun right in the middle of the head in the back with the band interwoven in the hair and tied. Bobby pins are used to hold the hair up. Some women get a bald spot where those bobby pins have been stuck in place for years.

The one thing that annoyed me the most about clothing was the dresses. They are long, dark-colored, and have to be long enough to reach down to the ankles with no exceptions. To make things worse, no buttons are allowed on the dresses; only straight pins can be used to keep it in proper place. However, girls under age nine can use buttons. Pins can hurt if not used properly. I pricked myself a million times!

Men are required to wear dark-colored pants with suspenders and a dark-colored shirt, and they are allowed to use hooks and eyes in place of buttons and zippers for the pants and jackets. Their shirts have buttons, though. Men really have it nice: no sweaty hands trying to put pins in place, no long hair to wash and fix up, no baby to carry in the womb every year. I always thought it would be just as fair if the men had to use straight pins, too, instead of buttons.

The men cut their hair in a Dutch-boy style, and there are a few rules when it comes to men's haircuts: they cannot have it so short that their ears show, and their bangs cannot be too short either. They only wear a brimmed hat while outside working, otherwise they do not need to keep their head covered like women do. If they are married, men wear a full beard with no mustache.

Even though the Amish uniform is old-fashioned, impractical, and uncomfortable, they would never consider becoming more modern because they believe it is disrespectful to their ancestors.

I remember outsiders and other modern Amish groups making fun of us, making me feel insecure; I reacted by pretending I was someone else and by becoming rebellious. The strict rules left me no room to breathe, which made me lash out in ways I otherwise would not have. I often thought I had a special privilege to break the rules, which happened most often when I was around Eli and his friends. My attitude became "I can do this or I can do that and the law won't touch me because I am Amish." This imagined privilege is why I felt so confident taking the truck for a ride. It was my way of being rebellious without caring about the consequences, as well as a way of escaping who I really was. At the time, I did not feel any remorse or guilt for my actions. I thought it was a cool thing to do, and so did my sisters, once the fear of getting caught passed.

When I look back on the stolen truck event now, I cannot believe I left the house that night, abandoning four little children while they slept. I remember walking towards the house in the darkness hoping the baby was not crying. If the Byler's knew the sly side of me, they would never have hired me in the first place. Or if my parents had known what thoughts played in my head, they would never have let me out of their sight. I was not a very good role model for my sisters.

My parents expected me to be a good role model when I stayed home from school to babysit. I was only eight years old then, in third grade, a very common age to take on that responsibility. Mem and Datt would take the youngest baby with them, but would leave three or four young ones for me to care for, including a one-year-old toddler. They went grocery shopping or to the flea market. Even though they would only be gone three or four hours, it felt like an entire week.

Staying inside the big white three-story farmhouse scared me, so I would take everyone outside to play. I always heard creepy noises in the house even though it was brand new. The house had four bedrooms upstairs, and the main floor contained the master bedroom along with a big living area, kitchen, and pantry. We used the basement for general storage and a place to stock canned goods.

I felt better outside, but I would make everyone hide behind the house or a tree whenever a vehicle drove by. One day a car pulled over and stopped in front of the house. It was a small golden brown station wagon, and to me it looked like the type of car a kidnapper would use. Friends had warned me there were two types of vehicles to watch out for: a station wagon, and any vehicle with an open sunroof. We all scurried into the house, locked all the doors, lowered the window blinds, and waited for over an hour until the car left. What a relief—we had not been kidnapped! I sequestered the little ones indoors for the rest of the day in case the car came back.

I always tried to be the brave one at home, and since I was the oldest of the girls, I was expected to be courageous. Sometimes my parents would visit the neighbors in the evening during the week. When they left, I took care of the kiddos. It scared me to be the one in charge when it started to get dark, so I would stand on the porch and yell as loud as possible, hoping Mem and Datt would hear me. In Ohio, before we moved to Missouri, we had neighbors all around us, but the neighbors my parents visited that evening lived about two miles away. My hollering never did any good; they came home when they were ready, not when I was.

Not only was I scared of the dark, I was also horrified when thunderstorms or tornadoes rolled through. It was not the storms I feared, but rather that one of the children would get too close to the chimney and stove. My parents had warned me that people died from standing or sitting too close to the chimney during a storm. We would even keep our dogs from hiding in this area, and yet it seemed like it was the first place they ran to when a storm roared in. Of course it turned out there was no truth to the warning, but at such a young age I not only believed it, I acted on it.

It seems every Amish family is on a mission to see who can raise the most children. My grandfather on my datt's side was best known as Gingerich Dowdy. He had twenty-one children, seventeen with his first wife, who died of cancer, and four with his second wife. On my mem's side, there were only ten children, although it is very typical for a family to have twelve to fifteen children. I did not get to know any of my grandparents very well, mostly because they were too scary. Gingerich Dowdy looked like he came from pure evil. If looks could kill, he would have been a mass murderer. He had a long crooked nose, a wrinkled face, and shoulder length gray hair that was always greasy and uncombed. He had one deaf and mentally challenged son, Noah—my uncle—whom he abused by beating or grabbing his beard and pulling him around like a dog. I could not stand being near his house because it would upset me.

I can remember one instance where Dowdy grabbed Noah by the beard at a bus station where the public could see it, but no one did anything about it. Soon after that, Noah came to stay at our house for a while. He was in his thirties at the time. The very first night after he arrived, I woke up to a crying sound from across the hallway, so I jumped out of bed to see what was wrong. Noah stood in the middle of the moonlit bedroom with his hand between his legs. My jaw dropped in disbelief. Since he was deaf, I did not know how to explain to him to go downstairs to use the outhouse, so I bolted down the dark stairs on my tip toes so I would not wake up anyone, ran out to the cold washhouse, and found a little dirty bucket. I ran back upstairs in less than a minute and handed Noah the bucket; he quit crying and motioned me to leave the room. I was only eight years old and proud that I could help Noah with his needs without having to wake up my parents.

I did not visit Gingerich Dowdy's house often, but when I did, I never saw Dowdy smile—he remained in a perpetual bad mood and always complained about something. I was thankful my datt had a sense of humor, and many Amish people liked him. I was even more thankful Datt never abused us like Dowdy did his kids. At the time, I was too young to see my datt's faults, but as I became much older he came across as lazy and unapproachable.

On the other hand, my mem's datt, who we called Miller Dowdy, never physically abused his children, but he was not a very friendly person either. He hardly ever smiled and was very bossy. I remember him hovering over my brother Jacob as he tried to fix a buggy, barking orders and telling him he did not know what he was doing. Miller Dowdy wore old round glasses and suspenders to keep his pants up. He looked like a typical Amish grandfather, unlike Gingerich Dowdy.

My parents had a total of fourteen children. I was around fifteen years old before I realized my mother actually carried the baby inside her body, and I had no idea what caused her to have a baby. Amish parents do not talk to their children about having a new baby on the way. Many times I would wake up in the morning and there would be a baby crying in the bedroom, which is how I found out I had a new brother or sister.

When I was around nine years old, I assumed that in order to have a baby, parents would choose from a long line of babies in a store and bring it home. I often wondered where I would be if they had not chosen me. I could not imagine being someone else's child. I thought of all my aunts and uncles and I would not have wanted them to be my mother or father.

During my third year in school, around the same time I stayed home to babysit, Anna, one of my best friends, told me that an airplane had flown over their house the night before and dropped a baby girl into the house. I believed her.

"How did the airplane know your parents wanted a baby?" I asked.

"Uh, I think the airplane just flies around and drops babies wherever they want to," Anna answered.

One day my curiosity got the best of me. "Hey," I said to Mem, "Why don't you and Daddy get a baby from an airplane like Anna's parents did?"

She looked up from the sewing machine where she was making a bonnet for my sister, Rhoda. She looked at me as though I had gone crazy. Instead of telling me anything different, though, she said, "I didn't know they got one from an airplane."

I was confused as to why Mem would not know anything about it if that was really where babies came from, but I was too young to question anything. In fact, my family did not encourage asking questions about anything, which became a big problem for me as I got older. Nonetheless, from then on, I watched for airplanes, hoping to see if my parents or our neighbors would get a new baby. I would lay out on the lawn for hours staring up into the sky, but after several months my curiosity wore off.

In fact, when I got older I did not want my parents to have any more babies as I realized how much work it was to take care of so many. They already had ten of them. Every time I heard an airplane buzzing over our house I would silently say, "Drop the baby somewhere else, we don't need it."

Some days I would complain about the gigantic piles of laundry we needed to wash, or the oodles of dishes in the sink that had to be cleaned three times a day. There was never a dull moment with so many siblings. One time Mem had enough of my whining and asked, "Well, what do you want me to do about all the work?"

"There are way too many kids," I retorted.

"Which one do you not want?" she asked, sounding disappointed.

After pondering her question, I realized all my siblings were too darn precious not to want them. "Umm, I–I want every one of them," I stammered.

I was ashamed of my complaining. I thought of each sister and brother carefully. Even though I had grown annoyed with all nine of them, the thought of giving away one child was unimaginable, because at the end of the day I enjoyed having them around. I was glad Mem put me in my place. She had four more children after that, and after putting my selfish pride away, I willingly welcomed them into the family.

§

I was born in Mount Eaton, Ohio and we moved five different times while in Ohio. My datt finally started a successful sawmill business, and I thought that with the nice house we lived in we would surely not move again, but we did. This time, my parents decided to leave Ohio altogether and relocate the whole family to northern Missouri in late winter 1998. I was almost 11 years old then, but I felt much older because of my family responsibilities.

The move to Missouri started badly. First, we were crammed into a drafty, freezing-cold trailer house. Then it snowed about four feet, which was more than we had ever seen, especially for the month of March. To make it worse, frigid cold crept into every part of the trailer. The trailer contained only a small wood stove used to heat the living area. Moving from a three-story house to a little two-bedroom trailer with a tiny kitchen was like taking six giant steps backwards in life. There was no room to put all the furniture so it stayed outside covered with a tarp.

About a month after we moved, Grandma Sarah, my mem's mother, died. Mem and Datt sent us to stay with our cousins so they could go back to Ohio for the funeral. Our cousins had just moved to Missouri too, but we did not know them very well and it made for a difficult week. I wished Grandma could have waited several more years to leave this earth, until we were at least settled into our new home. I was used to babysitting, but I was not used to doing it day and night for a week. We were all homesick by the time Mem and Datt returned.

Shortly after the move to Missouri I began to get irritated very easily with Amish life in general. One aspect of daily life which seemed to irritate me the most was having to ride three miles to school in a horse-drawn buggy, especially on cold days. The Amish community sprawled a far distance, so the schoolhouse was located where everyone had a fair amount to travel for school. There is nothing worse than riding in a buggy with a cold wind howling in from every direction. Six of us piled into a buggy at one time, and I felt sorry for the younger siblings because they had to endure the cold and long rides back and forth, just as I did. We did not have heaters in the buggy, just ice-cold seats to sit on and frozen blankets to cover up with.

Despite my irritation with traveling in the wintertime, I would actually get excited when we hitched two horses to a sleigh instead of a buggy. One particular time brings a smile to my face: it was our first day to hook up the sleigh and plenty of snow blanketed the gravel road. My oldest brother, Jacob, drove the sleigh. He was only thirteen, and just like any other teenager, he thought he was tough, but he soon learned otherwise. After a cold, dreary day at school, we could not wait to get home. We climbed into the sleigh and bundled in blankets while Jacob called to the horses. Shortly after we started heading home, Jacob let the frisky horses trot too fast around a corner and the sleigh flipped onto its side. The overturned sleigh threw us all into a big ditch filled with several feet of snow. The younger children started to cry immediately, but no one was hurt, just scared. Luckily, the horses stopped and stood still like nothing had happened. I do not know how we did it, since we were so small, but we all pitched in and managed to set the sleigh upright and continue home. We rode to school with the sleigh several more times after that adventure, but Jacob drove the horses slower around every corner.

However, it was not just the buggy rides to school that irritated me. As I got older, I grew more and more annoyed as my Amish life became more and more boring; there was just not enough going on to keep me occupied. Instead of acting like a young lady, as was expected of me, I began inventing ways to make life more interesting. As a result, I began to make mischief behind my parents' backs.

As I grew older and my responsibilities reached the full level of household duties, my younger sister, Rhoda, became old enough to help, and that is when she decided it was her turn to boss me around as I did to her when I babysat. Sometimes when I got in trouble, Rhoda attempted to provide the parental guidance she thought I needed.

Rhoda was one year younger than me and was a momma's girl. She always acted like she was older than me and she tried to boss me around; she got away with it most of time. Rhoda never got into any trouble that resulted in punishment. Mem even told me once that people in church often commented on how cute Rhoda was. After that, I knew I would never be Mem's favorite. Rhoda was a picture-perfect young lady. I envied her because it seemed like she had a free spirit and no guilty conscience to hide from the world. Except the one time when she threw away a little radio I secretly hid.

After several weeks of frantically searching for my radio, and dreading God had somehow taken it away from me to teach me a lesson, I feared I was doomed. Sarah was the only one who knew I kept the forbidden piece of electronics, and she was concerned that if we continued looking for it, God would punish us for sure. I had hidden the radio in the attic, and because it disappeared in the summer time, the attic sweltered from the blazing summer heat.

"Don't you think the radio just melted and disappeared up here?" Sarah asked with a red sweaty face, staring straight at me.

We had crawled up the stairs to the attic to look for the radio once more, but we did not make it all the way to the top before we turned around and climbed back down to the landing; it was just too hot.

"No Sarah," I replied. "If a radio melts then wouldn't all those boxes up there catch on fire?"

Then one day, after several months of searching and wondering what had happened to my radio, Rhoda overheard our conversation as Sarah and I continued trying to piece the puzzle together. She confessed she had thrown it in the ditch next to the road.

"Why in the world would you that?!" I roared, trying hard not grab her neck.

"It is evil to have a radio and you girls know better than to have one," she answered calmly, as if it was no big deal. "You should be glad I was trying to protect us."

"Protect us? What do you mean by that?" Sarah growled.

"I heard that the *Hau* can bring bad luck to the whole family when one of us does something we are not allowed to do," answered Rhoda sweetly. Hau means God, or the "Good Man," in German. In my family, there were certain things we did not speak about, and one of these was fear of causing God's retribution if we did not follow the rules. No one said those exact words, but there was a mutual understanding it could happen.

I did not say anything more to Rhoda. Instead, I snuck out to the ditch and found the radio where she had thrown it, but the rain had already ruined it. As I stomped the radio into the ground, I wondered what my sister really thought of me. I felt so guilty for having a radio when I knew it was wrong, and I could not help but agree with her that I was putting the whole family in danger. I prayed the Good Man would have mercy on my family, and if bad luck happened, I hoped it would only happen to me because it was my fault.

Even though having a radio was wrong, listening to music was my number-one passion. Many nights I lay in bed completely under the covers and listened to anything I could pick up. I did not know the difference between a country and pop rock station—as long as there was music I was happy. Understanding the words of a song was impossible for me: I had only learned a little bit of English in school, but not enough to let me enjoy the lyrics.

The music's rhythm comforted me, but it also terrified me because I worried someone would burst into my room without warning. With so many people in the house, there was no telling when someone would decide to pop into my room. There was no lock on the door, but if there had been, it would have only made me look suspicious if I had used it. Since I knew I was doing something wrong, I wondered if I would wake up the next day and still be in good health. I became convinced something was bound to happen to me. I feared listening to this music would result in bad luck, so sometimes I would crush and throw away my own radio. Then if nothing bad happened to me, I would find a way to secretly buy another one. Every time I purchased another radio I could feel the cashier staring a hole in me. I automatically assumed all cashiers and store employees had been forewarned by the Amish men to report if they saw someone buying anything we were not supposed to have.

Rhoda did not tell my parents about the radio she had thrown out, or there would have been consequences to pay. For that, I was grateful. But every time I got caught with one, Datt would preach to me about the sin I had brought down upon myself. Having a radio in Amish was forbidden, which was hard enough for me to understand, but asking questions did no good because no one would provide an answer that made any sense. I had gotten caught many times with a radio, and my parents would hold it over me for several days, and I would feel my household workload increase. They did not have to punish me because I already felt guilty enough for my actions. I was sure God was going to give me a disease, or I was going to end up in some sort of freak accident.

I knew Rhoda had her reasons for doing what she did, but she surprised me by taking care of the matter on her own. As I got older and my irritation with the Amish way of life increased, my position as a good role model for my siblings deteriorated. However, I had a feeling Rhoda would someday be a great mother to her own children, even if they did not come from airplanes. Now as I think back on Rhoda's faithfulness and dedication to the Amish rules, I wonder why I did not have that kind of commitment too. I stepped out of my comfort zone to find the one thing my heart was missing: freedom. Instead of getting married and raising a family like Rhoda will someday, I am now learning to support myself without the dominance of a man.

Chapter 3:

Life as a Teenager

*Trust that your soul has a plan even if
you can't see it all.*

~Deepak Chopra~

Sitting in a modern engine-driven combine gave me a high like I was on drugs or something. Never in my life had I thought I would be doing anything in a field without the use of horses, but the summer after I escaped from the Amish I jumped at the opportunity to work on a farm in North Dakota. I was thrilled to drive a combine to harvest wheat. Working with equipment other than horses was a new and exciting challenge for me, and I took the opportunity to do something crazy before I started a new semester in college.

I had no problem learning how to drive the enormous piece of machinery; I only weighed 105 pounds, which made me feel like a little rat sitting in the huge tractor. However, after a couple days of practice, I drove the combine like a pro. At home, the whole family would spread out into the wheat field and set up bundles of freshly-cut wheat in shocks (little huts). It was hard work to pick up and carry those bundles, but we had to do it so the bundles could dry out before being fed into the thrashing machine powered with a big engine with a long belt connected to the thrasher.

When I was still at home, I had always been more of an outside farm girl than a stay-in-the-house girl. I wondered how I could now drive a combine when I had all kinds of trouble guiding horses when I was younger. I loved being out in the barn milking the cows early in the mornings, or feeding the chickens and gathering eggs in the late afternoons. While I enjoyed those chores, I was also glad to hand those chores over to somebody else. In my house, the chores dribbled down the line as each child grew old enough to do them. The girls started by doing housework, such as cooking, cleaning, and taking care of babies, then graduated to doing chores out in the barn, which consisted mostly of milking cows and feeding chickens. The boys did the rest of the work, but they never helped with housework, which the Amish considered girls' work. Once my younger siblings grew old enough to take care of these kinds of chores, I began helping with my family's main income: weaving baskets.

Besides weaving baskets at the age of twelve, I got the part time job of driving a team of horses during the haying season. The idea thrilled me! However, my brothers were not too enthused because they thought I was just a flimsy sister who needed to stay in the house where women belonged.

On one hot summer day, I stood high on the wagon headboard driving a team of Belgian horses through the long rows of freshly-raked hay. I had to make sure the hay loader hooked onto the back of wagon was raking it up. Jacob, my younger brother, Sam, and the hired hand, Menno, stacked the loose hay with forks as it came up the loader. I wanted to prove to my brothers I was strong and could handle anything. Of course, when I was trying to prove my boyish skills, something always went wrong, and this time was no exception. While standing tall and breathing in the fresh smell of cut hay, something suddenly frightened the horses and they bolted. Unfortunately, my big girl panties were just not big enough to handle the spooked horses. I screamed for help while yanking the reigns with all my strength. Menno dashed forward from the back of the wagon and grabbed the lines from me, but it was too late. The huge load of hay slid off the wagon, dragging my brothers and I with it, burying us as we hit the ground.

No one got seriously hurt, just some bumps and bruises, but it shook us all up. The boys blamed me for making the horses run away. I do not know how I scared them, unless they saw my dress flapping around from the wind. More likely the boys did not like me driving, so they blamed me for the runaway regardless, so I would quit driving. So I did. I did not drive any more for the rest of the haying season, and the bad luck did not end there; it followed me around for the next several years.

§

The next incident occurred soon after I finished school, when I was around fourteen years old. Everyone only received an eighth-grade education, then we stayed home and worked full time. At fourteen, my parents allowed me to go to town without another adult to run errands. On this particular day I had to go to the hardware store to buy some supplies for our basket shop. I took my two-year-old sister, Lizzie, with me so Mem could get a little break.

I drove a horse named Smokey. He was supposed to be safe for the girls to drive, but as he walked through town he suddenly spied a water sprinkler in someone's yard. With no warning, he threw his head up and took off galloping down the street. This was so unexpected I could not get control of him soon enough. It did not matter how hard I pulled on the reigns, Smokey did not slow down. It seemed like he held the bridle bit between his teeth so he would not feel it when I pulled on the lines. *What a smart horse*, I thought.

We flew through a stop sign with a blur and crossed a busy highway so fast I did not have time to scream at the car we almost smacked into. Not that screaming would have done any good. Smokey ran straight into the backyard, turning just enough to miss the car sitting in the driveway and the corner of the garage. The horse almost ran into a clothesline, but he managed to stop short. Lizzie fell sideways at the sudden stop and bumped her head against the side of the seat frame. It jerked my head so badly it took me a second to realize what had just happened. Smokey stood quietly, and I realized if he had not stopped short of the clothesline, the damage that would have caused would have been on a whole different level.

As I came to my senses, I had to figure out how to calm down my hysterically-crying little sister. Smokey stood very still and looked around nervously. His hindquarters shook as if he thought I was going to punish him with the buggy whip. I spoke to him gently to calm him down. Smokey had kicked grass up from the lawn, exposing dirt where the horse's feet had scraped it away.

As Lizzie calmed down, I assessed the situation: because of the size of the yard and the proximity of the house and the clothesline, there was no way I could turn around or back out the buggy. My next option was to unhitch the horse. However, I could not climb down from the buggy and leave Lizzie sitting by herself, and if I took her with me, I could not hold on to Smokey. I closed my eyes and hoped when I opened them again I would wake up in bed and this would only be a bad dream. Unfortunately, when I opened my eyes again the bad situation was as real as ever.

I glanced toward the house and saw a man standing at the back door. He was on the phone. *Yikes! He is already calling the police!* I thought. He disappeared back into the house. *This is not good. He is not even going to see if I need help.* During a time like this it would have been nice to have a cell phone to call my parents for help. *Do not even think about phones right now, think, think, think of a way to get out.* A few minutes later the man left his house and walked over to the buggy.

"I apologize for not coming sooner," he said. "I was on an important call when I saw this horse and buggy flying into the yard."

My chest hurt from my heart beating so fast, and my nerves sang with the tension of the situation. "So did you call the police?" I asked in a scared voice, almost choking.

He looked at me over the top of his glasses and smiled. "There is no need to get police involved," he said. "I can help you."

"I-I- I am sorry this happened," I stammered. "Something scared the horse and he made a mad dash down the street."

"I understand," he said, still looking at me over the rim of his glasses. "Don't be sorry, accidents happen all the time and you and your sister are very lucky girls that you didn't get hit crossing the highway."

I was relieved he was one of the few city people who did not mind Amish people and their horses. At the time, some people in the town complained about the horse poop on the city streets, and they even tried to pass a city law requiring horses to wear diapers. The Amish elders did not agree with it, so it never happened. As a result, some people were not very friendly with the Amish anymore.

The man held on to Smokey while I unhitched him from the buggy. I could not turn the cart around by myself so we tied Smokey to the clothesline post. With the man's help, we turned the buggy around and hitched Smokey to it again.

As soon as we got back on the road, Smokey was very skittish; any little noise made him jump. I was scared to drive home, especially since I was still in town. I needed to make one more stop at the grocery store, but I was not about to take the risk of Smokey acting up again. I decided it would be best to turn around and go back home and hope Mem would not be too upset for not bringing home the groceries.

That night I told my family what had happened, but they did not seem to grasp the idea of how scary it had been to fly across a busy highway and mess up a stranger's back yard.

"I am not very happy about it since it's so far to town and we are pretty busy here at home," Mem said while peeling potatoes for supper at the kitchen sink, "but I guess we will go tomorrow again to get groceries."

Datt stood at the kitchen door smoking his pipe, and the look on his face told me he thought I was a reckless person. Finally, after staring at me for what seemed like ten minutes, he said, "You probably weren't minding your business or it wouldn't have happened."

I wanted to say, *Okay whatever you say, Datt*, but I kept my mouth shut. There was no use trying to explain why it had happened; whenever he puffed his pipe he always seemed to drift off with the smoke to a faraway land. I had my baby sister with me, so of course I was minding my business. I did not want something to happen to her. I felt so sorry for Lizzie. She had been scared out of her skin, and on the way home I had made her sit close to me to help her feel comfortable again.

§

It was not long before another incident made me begin to wonder if Datt was right about me not paying attention to my surroundings. This incident did not involve traffic or a runaway horse, but rather a mailbox. That time I drove an ugly, stupid, and stubborn horse named Minnie. No one liked to drive Minnie, and on that particular day she walked extra slow. I did not blame her, though—she had twelve miles to get me where I was going.

I had to go to my datt's twin brother Jacob's family to help them prepare for the church service that Sunday. The services rotated from one family's house to the next, and it was tradition the girls help close relatives get ready for church on one day during the week.

Preparing to have a church service at our house usually took a whole week. The house had to be cleaned from top to bottom, not only because we wanted it clean, but also so people would not complain about spotting a speck of dirt, which would have been embarrassing.

After completing the cleaning by Wednesday, the baking started on Thursday. The women began by baking bread to make the bean soup for Sunday's dinner. It took roughly twelve loaves just for the soup, and another twelve for lunch to eat with jams and jelly. On Friday they made buttermilk cookies and snitz (dried apple) pies, which is standard Amish practice. The cookies and pies were set aside for the little children to snack on during the church service. The adults would eat whatever was left over, after the dishes were washed. The men never helped with the dishes, but yet they got a snack too. I never could understand that concept.

I was not excited about helping my Uncle's family because I was not enthusiastic about cleaning and baking at someone else's house when we could not even keep up at home. But I went anyway.

About an hour after I left home, I was driving along the shoulder of a busy highway when it started to rain. When I reached down to grab a cover off the floorboard, Minnie edged farther onto the shoulder of the road, pulling the cart with her. When I looked up again, the front wheel rolled right up to a mailbox shaped like a pig. I quickly jerked the lines to stop the horse, but it was too late: I hit the piggy mailbox with a hard crunch. The lid, shaped as the pig's nose, fell open, the cover twisted, and the whole mailbox rotated sideways with a loud squeal.

I did not know what to do. All the houses were on the opposite side of the road, so I did not think anyone saw the accident, so I kept on driving. I knew everyone would realize a buggy hit the mailbox because the wagon wheels left fresh tracks in the moist sand leading away from the twisted pig. I did not see any other buggies on the road, so I thought I would have a good chance no one would ever find out who did it. They would especially not suspect it was me.

Once I got to my Uncle Jacob's house, the whole morning seemed out of whack. I tried to concentrate on helping my cousins clean the wooden floors and windows upstairs, but the image of the mailbox would not leave me alone. *What should I do about it?* I worried.

While we sat around the table eating lunch, Uncle Jacob answered my question when he asked, out of the blue, if I had hit a mailbox on the big highway. He took a big bite of mashed potatoes and continued, "I just thought it might have been you since you were the last person on the road before me."

I felt my face turn beet red. I had not expected him to ask me that question. He had been in town that morning and apparently had not been too far behind me as he drove home. Of course, I had to tell him the truth—there was no way to hide my guilt-flushed face.

"Yeah, it was me that hit the mailbox," I said. I wished I could disappear into a hole, like groundhogs do.

"Be sure to tell your Datt about it because he needs to go talk to the owners and offer to fix it," he said calmly.

There was no way I could tell my datt about it. After what had happened six month ago with Smokey, he would really question my ability to drive anymore.

"I will let him know," I said after a long pause.

The rest of my day was just horrible; I rode myself thinking about how I had ruined someone else's mailbox. Some English people on this side of town did not even like the Amish, and I wondered if the owners of that piggy mailbox could be one of them. Amish-haters had smashed our own mailbox several times in the past. In fact, about a year after we had moved to Missouri, some young guys had driven by our place at night on several occasions and destroyed the mailbox. They had even gone as far as backing into the corner of our house to scare us. I remember lying awake at night scared, wondering if someone could hate the Amish enough to set our house on fire. For just a few seconds, I felt smug that I had the opportunity to smash someone else's mailbox because of what had happened to ours. I had been taught not to take revenge, but as long as I was only thinking those kinds of thoughts and not telling anyone about them, I thought I would be fine.

I drove home by a different route that evening so I would not have to face the damaged piggy. I did not want to see if the owners had already discovered it. In a way, I was mad with myself, but I tried to find a way to blame the incident on my datt. He should have never bought such a stubborn little horse, especially since no one liked her. Deep down I knew I was the only one to blame, but at the time, it felt better to blame it on someone else.

I decided not to tell my parents what had happened that day because I did not want to face Datt's judgment. My heart sank a week later when Uncle Jacob and his wife came to visit and catch up on gossip. I feared them telling my parents, so I avoided them in case my presence accidentally reminded them of what had happened. I was almost certain Uncle Jacob would not forget, but every time he came around I would hide so as not to jog his memory. After each visit from his brother, I was afraid Datt would seek me out and ask me about it. After all, I had only made the situation worse by not only hiding the fact I hit the mailbox, but also because I did not confess to him at once. Life went on, however, and I never heard another word about that day, but I carried the burden for a whole year before I grew confident Datt was not ever going to find out.

§

The harvesting in North Dakota ended and I headed back to Texas, where it was almost time for me to start my next chapter in life. I had a feeling the days of working in the fields were over, but I was excited to finally start going to college. Harvesting acres and acres of wheat gave me plenty of time to think about my childhood, especially my teenage years. Being free reminded me that God was always looking out for me whether I knew it or not, and He had guided me to the outside world where He meant for me to be. Thinking about the freedom I now have brought tears to my eyes. I thanked God for the chance to drive a combine, and I compared it to the time when I was just a farm girl at home.

I was sixteen years old and Amish tradition dictated girls should not do fieldwork. But I did not care—I loved it! My two oldest brothers, Jacob and Sammie, did not like farming. So Jacob got a job at an Amish sawmill business making slats for pallets. I traded jobs with Sammie when he complained about having to work in the fields to get ready for spring planting. For my part, I was not content sitting in the shop all day long making baskets. Sammie promised he would try his best to do my job so Mem would not miss my work too much. Basket sales produced our main household income, and the women did most of the weaving. Datt smoked his pipe all day long and expected things to get done without his help. I thought the reason he had so many children was for them to do the work and serve him like a king, as was customary for Amish families.

As Sammie took over my job weaving baskets, I jumped into his job plowing the fields. It did not take me long to learn how to plow with a John Deere one-bottom plow pulled by four big Belgian horses. I do not know how I decided I could handle four horses when I had had problems with just one, but the fact that Datt trusted me with his big babies was shocking. Nevertheless, things started out smoothly and I was able to keep it like that.

I did not have much freedom as an Amish girl, so being in the field all alone, all day long is like being on a vacation. No one bossed me around; in fact, I bossed the horses around. That gave me a great feeling of satisfaction, and suddenly I realized how Rhoda must have felt. I did not have to do much bossing though—the horses knew what they were supposed to do. I looked up at the blue sky and said thank you to the Good Man for giving me the opportunity to be out here all alone, a half mile from home.

As soon as I thought I had the world by the tail, Rhoda decided she wanted her turn at the plow too. Of course, I had to give in and let her try. In our family we had a set age for when we were old enough to do certain work, but everything I did, Rhoda got to do too. She did not have to wait until she was old enough. As soon as I was old enough to bake pies, which was about the only thing I enjoyed doing in the kitchen, Rhoda took it away from me. Now she wanted to start plowing, but there was no way I would let her take that away from me too. Unfortunately, I had no control over it, and since my parents favored her, and whatever they said happened, they agreed Rhoda was old enough to plow.

I did not have to fret too long, though, because Rhoda gave up the first hour in the fields. She could not coax the horses to move forward; no matter what she did to get them to move, they would not listen. I did not watch her that day, but I heard the horses somehow got tangled up in the lines and harness. It made me happy Rhoda was now officially not a farm girl. I got my job back and I plowed for the next ten days, excluding Sunday. I never tired of it. I enjoyed talking to the horses, praising them for messing up Rhoda's chances for my sake. When the horses rested, I jumped off the plow and walked barefooted on the moist soil. The freshly-turned sod felt soft and cool under my bare feet. My contentment and joy came to an abrupt end when my menstrual cycle arrived and Mem would not let me go out to the fields to plow anymore.

§

I hated when this part of the month came. Amish rules required women to take it easy during their menstrual cycle, stay in the house, and do only light housework. This was especially hard for me during the summer months when there was so much to do outside. During the summer, everyone went barefoot except when that dreaded time of the month hit; I then had to wear shoes for a whole week.

My siblings would ask, "Why are you wearing shoes?" and I could not answer because it was not my place to explain. No one ever talked to me about it, so why should I talk to them about it?

I had no clue what was happening the first time I started bleeding at age eleven. I thought I was deathly ill. I did not feel comfortable enough to tell Mem about it, but after the second day of freaking out, I finally broke down.

"Oh yeah," she said, "you will start being a '*gluk*' every month now." (*Gluk* means the same as a hen setting on eggs to hatch them).

She showed me some Kotex pads and told me to wear them.

"By the way, tell me every time you are a *gluk*," she added, before going back to the sewing machine.

I did not know what to think. *Gluk*? What a terrible word. *Why do I have to tell her?* I felt embarrassed, but for what? I had many questions, but asking them was something I could not easily do. My life changed after that, and every time my period started I had to stay home from school for two days, and Mem did not give me any chores requiring too much hard work. I once heard from a friend that if women did not take care of themselves while on their periods, they got very sick and would eventually become handicapped.

After a couple more periods, I started to wonder if all mothers did not inform their daughters about how their bodies would change into bloody monsters for one week every month. It scared me to death when I saw Rhoda wearing shoes one hot summer day. *Oh no, I am her big sister. Was I supposed to warn her before she got that far? I do not know.* I suspect Rhoda might have known a little about it because she had seen me suffer through it for a year. She did not look worried about it at all. She always had a way of taking everything in stride. Nonetheless, I felt sorry for her.

§

Besides being old enough to work in the fields with horses, and drive into town for shopping, I was also old enough to become a hired maid. Being a teenage girl is like being a slave mother to children of other families. Before girls got married, they had a chance to be hired out to other families needing help with a newborn baby, or needing baby sitters while the parents visited their families and friends out of town.

I worked for an Amish family with eight children. I got paid $1.50 a day, but I had to relinquish the pay to my parents; I was not allowed to keep any money until I turned twenty-one. I had some experience from helping the neighbors, but this time the family lived eighteen miles away, a two-hour drive with horse and buggy. I loved being away from home any chance I had; however, this time I was anything but enthusiastic.

The parents left for Michigan to visit family and friends, and planned to be gone for over two weeks. They took their two-year-old son, but they left me to take care of an eight-month-old baby named Edna and six other children. The oldest attended fifth grade.

Talk about growing up fast! I was only seventeen at the time. I had to pack my sweet girl looks away and put on a tough momma face. I thought I knew everything about raising kids from babysitting my own siblings, but when I tried caring for someone else's children, my little world got turned on its head.

In addition to watching the kids, I had to cook three meals a day, do the laundry, milk the cows, feed chickens, bottle-feed two small Holstein calves, make applesauce, can pears, pack lunches, and get the kids off to school. The list went on and on. A hired hand did the chores in the mornings so I could stay in the house to make breakfast and help get the rowdy children ready for school. At first, I thought it would be easy to get everything done each day if I made a list. Was I ever so wrong! I could never predict how each day would turn out. Looking back on it, I have to say this experience helped prepare me for the realities of life!

An endless pile of clothes to wash overflowed the washroom the first Monday after the parents left. I thought for sure I was going insane. I wanted to pack up the kids and take them to our house until their parents returned. It would have been better than washing clothes. I had a feeling the mother purposely did not do laundry the week before because she knew the hired maid would do it. A lot people lived at our house, yet never in my life had I seen such a big pile of clothes to wash. I did laundry from eight o'clock in the morning until five o'clock that evening. I lost my voice that day from the stress—my body had a weird way of reacting to it.

Amish have washing machines hooked up to small gasoline engines, but the water must be heated in a big kettle and carried to the washing machine. After the clothes have swirled in the water long enough, they are removed one-by-one and fed through a wringer to squeeze out the excess water.

I had to hang each piece of clothing on clotheslines to dry, and the poor little baby constantly cried that day while I washed clothes. The next day she was sick. She always cried during the night, keeping me up until I was almost in tears. I remembered to throw some regular table salt in her bed to keep her from getting too homesick. As I got a saltshaker and poured salt on the entire mattress, I wondered how on earth anyone would believe it really worked. It was something I used to do for my siblings when my parents left for more than a week. I do not think it helped, but I was desperate to find a solution and was willing to try anything.

If taking care of the household duties was not enough, the family had also asked me to take care of selling the farm's eggs. I had to wash eggs each day to make sure they were ready to sell if customers stopped by. I did not like it when someone stopped, but it happened several times a day and I had to drop everything to tend to the customers. One day, flour from making bread dough covered me from head to foot when someone knocked on the door. *I do not have time for this,* I thought impatiently, but I quickly dropped everything and wiped my hands. As I headed to the door, baby Edna started crying. I scooped her up from the dirty floor and answered the door.

"Hello," I said to an old man patiently waiting on the front steps.

He stared at me for a long second. I began to get nervous as I wondered what was wrong.

Then a smile broke on his face and he reached into his pocket, pulled out a clean handkerchief, and said, "You have something white smeared all over your face."

"Ya, it is probably white flour," I replied. "I am trying to make bread and the baby keeps crying so my hands are all over the place."

He gently wiped my face with the clean-scented handkerchief, then he asked where the parents were.

"They went out of town and I am staying with the kids."

"My goodness, don't you need a sitter for yourself?" He looked surprised. "No offense, but you look like a twelve-year-old."

"With these children there should be more than one babysitter," I laughed. "I am older than twelve, but I might as well not be."

"Yes, I feel for you, I have been here many times and I know how it goes around here. If I knew where the eggs are I could save you some energy and get them myself."

"I can get them for you. It is no problem."

I scurried down to the basement with the baby still in my arms. I came back with the three-dozen eggs he asked for.

He surprised me by saying, "If you pray a lot, things will go smoother for you."

I always pray silently, and nothing ever seems to change, I thought to myself rather angrily. *Maybe I am doing it wrong.* I smiled politely and said, "I will pray more often."

I watched him walk across the lawn to his rundown Dodge pickup. He had a slight limp and walked bow-legged. I wondered if he told me to pray because he thought Amish do not pray, or if he actually thought I looked pretty rough. I searched for a mirror, and my reflection confirmed the latter: I looked exhausted, and my greenish eyes stared back at me, red and sunken from lack of sleep. A shock of brunette hair hung out from under the bonnet sitting askew on my head, and white flour smeared across my pale cheeks as if I had a run-in at a flourmill. I was the only one in my family who prayed that I knew of, except for Datt, who said a silent prayer before and after each meal.

Each child I babysat had been given a list of chores to do when they got home from school, but after the second day they all decided to ignore them. They stomped through the door when they got home, threw their lunch buckets on the floor in front of the sink, and ran outside to play or fight with each other. The kids fought a lot, making my life a living hell. I tried to keep peace between them, but they would not listen. After all, to them I was nobody. Every time I asked them to play with the baby or carry wood for the cook stove, they jostled to figure out whose turn it was, and that resulted in total chaos. Compared to these rowdy and noisy kids, my siblings were perfect angels, even though they fought sometimes too.

I knew from living in the same community as this family that the children experienced much more physical and emotional abuse than my brothers and sisters ever did. I concluded that, since the parents were not home, the kids wanted a break from their hectic days and I felt a little sorry for them.

During this hectic two weeks I always had dishes to wash, floors to sweep, dirty diapers to change, and messes to clean up. I welcomed a dull moment, but none showed up, not even at night. Each night, while I held the baby and rocked her to sleep, I wondered how in the world I got myself into this. This experience was very far from the life I wanted. I already stood on the verge of a nervous breakdown from my days at home, and I knew if I continued to stay Amish, I would be expected to go work for other families or become a schoolteacher. Taking care of other people's households and children was a way of preparing for, and learning the values of, being a housewife. Then *boom!* Before I knew what hit me it would be time to get married and start my own family. Being an Amish woman, there was no time to be just me and enjoy life. I began to realize I wanted no part of it. I wanted to enjoy some freedom before I started my own family, and if I ended up having kids, I wanted to raise them in a different environment. How could parents even think young girls could take on such a responsibility of being both the mother and father of their unruly children?

I looked at the sweet, innocent baby girl sleeping peacefully in my lap and decided I needed to quit thinking all the negative thoughts and go to bed myself. It was already midnight and I was so burned out I could have cried myself to sleep, but I kept my emotions together as best I could. In five hours it would be time to get up and do it all over again.

Not only was babysitting someone else's children an emotional roller coaster, but the fact I was in turmoil ever since I started dating and going to church singings made life so much more miserable. *Teenage life should not be this difficult*, I thought as I laid the baby in her crib. *Something has got to change.*

Chapter 4:

What Does "No" Mean?

*Keep some room in your heart for
the unimaginable.*

~Mary Oliver~

If I base my life upon others' expectations, I will never be happy. Or I will never be human. Of course, fulfilling others' expectations will make them happy, and I should be happy because of their happiness, right? No. Happiness comes from within a person who has the opportunity to pursue exactly what they envision their life to be. When I was a child I did not want to envision my life as an adult, but I could not run away from it. After I accepted that I would become an adult no matter what, I finally found happiness several years later in a different identity. I just had to pursue something from within me until I came to the well where Jesus was handing out living water.

Becoming an adult and being old enough to date became my worst nightmare. It all hit me suddenly one Monday morning as the family gathered at the table as usual to eat breakfast. Datt said the prayer silently while we folded our hands under the table and bowed our heads. I peeked at Jacob and could not help noticing he was having a hard time waking up. His eyes drifted shut and his head bobbed forward and backward like a bird as he tried to keep himself awake long enough to fix a plate of eggs and pancakes.

He had come home early that morning—I heard him creep up the stairs and tiptoe into his bedroom about an hour before it was time to get up, and I suspected he had a date with someone last night, after the singings. It was not the first time he had come home late, but most of the time he was out late only on Saturday nights, not Sunday, too. He never uttered a word about what he did when he was gone, and he was not supposed to tell me anything until I reached the proper age of sixteen-and-a-half. I selfishly hoped he would not be going steady with a girl when I joined in the singings. I wanted him to be there for guidance when I started dating.

While trying to eat breakfast my mind churned on the dating and socializing confusion. I was almost old enough to start dating, stay out late on Sundays after church, and attend the singings. Many different Amish groups might call this *rumspringa*—the season of a teenager's life when rules are eased a bit, including more loosely-defined dating rituals. However, our little version of *rumspringa* was not nearly as easy and enjoyable as it sounds because, no matter what, someone would always be judging and complaining.

As I mentioned earlier, my Amish community did not allow *rumspringa,* and I do not remember hearing about this term when I started dating. Our parents taught us from a very early age what we could and could not do. Guys were allowed to go out on Saturday and Sunday nights. Sunday was the only time the girls were allowed to socialize, except for the few holidays we celebrated. Girls were not allowed to go out together either; there was no such thing as a "girls' day out." Girls were not allowed to get their nails and hair done or buy clothes, jewelry, purses or anything else girls enjoy doing together. Amish girls had nothing exciting in life to look forward to except getting married and raising a family. For me, that kind of future was not something I looked forward to. The Amish expected women to remain submissive; it was the only proper way for women to act. Women had always been submissive, therefore they always would be.

I also did not look forward to dating because the time would arrive for me to be baptized as well. I already had a hard enough time understanding why we even went to church let alone why the community expected us to get baptized. By the time I was well over sixteen, my life had become so confusing. Everyone else my age seemed to enjoy going to church and becoming a mature young adult. Everyone except me. I could not help but feel guilty about it: I did not want to commit to a normal Amish girl's lifestyle, and I longed to be free from any rules and commands. The Amish expected me to follow their ways without asking questions as I prepared to become a submissive member of the church by the age of eighteen. I was not ready to do that. Somehow I felt I would be punished for having those thoughts. I knew my parents would not be happy if they ever found out how I really felt about the Amish religion.

The Amish controlled the young generation so much it made it almost impossible not to feel guilty thinking about worldly desires or, even worse yet, making an escape. As long as baptism had not taken place, then the shunning a person experiences after he or she leaves the community is less severe.

To be baptized in the Amish church means a lifetime vow to uphold the discipline of the church. Amish youth get baptized at age eighteen, and then are expected to act as grown-up adults, being submissive to the rules. I truthfully could not make such a promise. I was too rebellious and wanted way more than Amish life could ever offer me.

The boys and girls preparing for baptism have to visit the preachers upstairs in a private room every Sunday morning while the first songs are being sung at church. Even after baptism, I never heard anyone talking about the experience during the eighteen-week process. I do not even know what the preachers talk about when young people visit them upstairs. I never asked my brothers and sisters either, and, of course, they did not offer to tell me. It is as if no one wants to break the silence for fear of being punished by God. I just knew that if I got baptized I would miss out on so many opportunities in life.

Somehow Jacob managed to finish his breakfast that morning, and I managed to further reinforce my desire to not be baptized. Later, after Jacob had gone to work, I started my task-filled week of making baskets in the shop. As I worked, I thought how graceful Jacob was not complaining of being tired after staying out all night. On the heels of that thought came the uncomfortable knowledge that, by next Sunday, the community and my family expected me to join the singings and start dating. Other people knew I was old enough, and I already felt the pressure to begin what was expected. I did not know how I would handle it because I would be taking a step closer to becoming an adult, or at least acting like one. I wanted to talk to Jacob about his thoughts on the church and the singings, but I felt awkward about it. He probably did not even question where his life was going, like I did.

During church service the previous day, I had trouble staying awake while sitting in the pew and listening to the preacher. To be honest, I really had not listened at all because I had no clue what he was saying. After three hours subjected to the drone of unintelligible words, I got far too bored. Church always felt this way because the Amish Bible is in a different German language than the language we spoke in everyday life; this frustrated me. Once I said something to Datt about not comprehending what was being preached at church. His response: it would eventually come to me if I tried harder. Tried harder? Really? My family never talked about God openly, so I was not even sure what to believe in. I would wonder *is there a God or am I just listening to man-made rules?* By the time I reached dating age, I became aware that some of the rules, in fact, were not in the Bible.

I often wondered where many of the Amish practices had come from, such as why the women had to wear long dresses and keep their hair covered. Church days were even worse. Sunday mornings were an extra special day for Amish women, as they have to get up early to dress their children for church. It was always crucial for my sisters and me to wear our best Sunday dress with a starched white apron and cape. The boys had to wear their best Sunday pants with a white collared shirt. We had to make sure everything fit just right because there were so many people with piercing eyes just hoping to find fault with someone, so they could complain. People were very judgmental, especially elderly women who had nothing better to do. I always assumed people who judged the most had a miserable life and had no intentions of letting someone else have it any better than they did.

The church was such a big tradition, and in our household there was never a reason to skip a Sunday unless someone was sick; we had to go, no matter what.

For everything in preparation for a church service there was a rule, and those rules never changed, including where people were supposed to sit. The men entered the house and sat according to age, the elderly first. The married men sat in the living room on one side. On the other side sat one row of the oldest ladies. Then the girls who were not married yet sat in front of them, facing the men. The young boys sat in front of the girls, also facing the married men. The rest of the people sat in the kitchen, including all the little children sitting with their mothers.

Church usually started at nine o'clock Sunday morning, and ended at 12:30 Sunday afternoon. Then, by the time everyone had eaten the usual meal of *gma sup* (church soup) made of milk, butter, beans, and bread, with sides dishes of red beets and pickles, it was about three o'clock. I always wondered why nobody ever changed the menu—eating the same thing every Sunday went beyond getting old for me. I did not dare ask for a change, because I figured the food had some sacred meaning and I did not want to be the girl that put her faith in jeopardy.

After lunch had been served, the young girls and women had the task of washing the huge pile of dishes and drying them by hand, plate-by-plate and fork-by-fork. The men had their lives pretty much cut out for themselves; they did not have to do a darn thing after service. They could visit and have a good time outside while the women took care of all the cooking, dishwashing, and taking care of crying children.

As I got older, I realized the church leaders were their own legal authorities, and they expected the members to follow the process without question. Most of the people were too ignorant to realize self-serving men from generations ago dictated their form of religion. This would have been easier to accept if the church leaders—and consequently parents following church tradition—did not brainwash young children into thinking that by not following the rules they were not right with God. I often felt this was the case with me since I was such a rule breaker.

When I asked about the rules, Datt would tell me the church followed demands written in the Bible. But I had plenty of questions whose answers could never be found in the Bible. Why couldn't we have a flush toilet? Why couldn't we have electricity? Why couldn't we hire a driver to take us to town to run errands? Why did the walls in a house always have to be white? Why was it forbidden to get any education past eighth grade? Why was a hand water pump installed by the sink where the men washed their hands, but there could not be one at the sink where the women washed dishes? I gave up hope that my questions would ever be answered. The only response I ever got was "This is the way it has always been and God will punish us if we do otherwise." For a long time I believed it. Maybe the Bible could not answer those questions, but deep down in my heart I knew that if we did anything different from what we had always done, it would be considered "worldly desires."

As I continued to struggle with a life that did not fulfill me, I embarked on a new dilemma as the dating game was about to start. As soon as I reached the proper age of sixteen-and-a-half, other people pressured me to join in the singings. I did not have a choice. I eventually decided to at least pretend as if I wanted to start so no one would become suspicious of me and start gossiping about my dislike of these traditions.

One Sunday morning, after I washed the breakfast dishes and finished dressing for church, I nervously ran downstairs and walked into the living room where my parents prepared for the day. It was a tradition to ask your parents' permission to join the singings. I had always felt more comfortable with Mem, so I asked her. She smiled and said, "You have to ask your Datt."

"That response sounds familiar and I hate it," I muttered. "I swear when I have children that phrase will be very limited."

Mem appeared rather happy that her oldest daughter was finally ready to take this next step in life. Datt sat in his usual chair in the living room, smoking his pipe. I did not think I even had to ask—he had heard me talking to Mem.

He stared at me for what seemed like an eternity. "Ahhemm," he cleared his throat, then said, "I wasn't planning on letting you start yet, but since you have been behaving well lately I guess it is all right if you stay for the singings."

Thick smoke curled from his pipe and I saw, very dimly, the hint of a smile cracking his face. My parents seemed unusually happy about my decision. I wondered why. Datt was right about my behaving well lately, only because I knew if I did not, it would cause me to start late in the singings, then everyone would find out why. I could not live with myself when people gossiped behind my back, or worse, judged me. If someone got into trouble, parents could punish their child by banning them from going to the singings for two or three Sundays. However, the real punishment was not missing the singings, it was the shame brought on by other people finding out the reason behind the punishment.

§

My first time at the singings started great that evening, and my nerves were much calmer than I expected. Everyone gathered around a long table in the kitchen, oil lamps glowing as we sang songs. The boys sat on one side of the table and the girls on the other. No music accompanied the singing, and we sung every song in German. A solo singer led every first word of each line, then we all pitched in to finish the rest of the line. Some of the singers really showed off their talent, but not me. As well as the evening started I still would rather have been home milking a cow than being there trying to avoid the young men's stares as they wondered if they could give me a ride home.

The singings usually finished at 9:00 in the evening, after which the young men hitched their horses to their buggies. Then those who had a girlfriend drove her home personally. The guys who did not have a girlfriend usually offered to take their cousins or neighbors home. Typically, however, several guys would get together to decide which singles should be paired up for a date. They played matchmaker and negotiated with the chosen guy and girl. They acted as middlemen, not allowing the guy to ask the girl for a date personally. Once the guy agreed to take one particular girl, the chosen girl had no choice but to go along with it unless she had a good excuse why she could not have a date with him. Those excuses were very hard to come up with.

As my bad luck would have it, I found out Jacob was going steady with a girl, which meant he would not be able to take me back home. I was disappointed. I had never gotten the chance to spend any time with him before I started going to the singings, and I longed to have a conversation with him about what to expect. That night I wanted to feel like I had an older brother who wanted to take care of his sister.

As it turned out, no one chose me for a date so my cousin Eli took me back home that night. I got to my room about midnight, and soon after, Jacob arrived home too. As I heard the squeaks on the stairs from Jacob trying to sneak in without waking anyone, I hoped he would come to my room and ask me about my first Sunday night experience, but he did not. My brother was very kindhearted, but something our family did not exercise was good communication skills. I do not know why I expected my brother to talk to me when I knew it was not what our family did. We were expected to just be silent and figure things out as they came along. My frustration with this silence only grew stronger as I got older.

Still fully clothed in my uncomfortable Sunday dress, I laid my weary body down on my bed and stared into the darkness. *Oh Lord, I am so exhausted*, I thought. I did not need any help when it came to breaking the rules and buying a forbidden radio, but when it came to taking life seriously, I longed to have someone to talk to. Many of my girlfriends were a little older than me so they got a head start, but it did not seem like they had any questions about life in general. They went with the flow, and I tried it too, but keeping questions bottled up tightly did not work well for me. *What is wrong with me?* I tried to be happy, but deep down in my heart I was crying.

The thought of dating scared me; I had no clue what to expect on a date. All I knew was the guy would give the girl a ride home then stay with her in her room on Saturday or Sunday nights. If a guy and girl decided to start dating, they could only spend one night together every two weeks. Although I knew these things, the question still remained: *What do they do while they are together?* I did not have any older sisters to learn from, and my mother never talked to me about anything. I did not think it would do any good to ask her because I would get the familiar answer of "you'll learn on your own someday." It stressed me out more telling Mem what I was thinking than keeping it to myself. Finally I rose from my bed, changed into my nightdress, and blew out the soft yellow flames in the oil lamp. I thought they were trying to show me a glimmer of hope as the flickering flame died. Exhausted by my first evening out, I crawled into bed and soon fell asleep.

§

The next week passed as usual: work, work, and more work. Another miserable Sunday came and went, complete with the singings. That next Monday morning I wove baskets as usual with Mem and my sisters. Sarah and Amanda brightened the shop with their humorous, silly selves. Usually I loved to laugh and joke with them, but I hardly noticed them because of how tired I was from the night before. This was the busiest time of the year: people always seemed to travel a lot during Fourth of July, and our baskets were a hot item at the roadside stand. In addition, orders had come through the mail more than ever, and we could hardly keep up. I did not have time to be tired and I wanted to be like my big brother and not complain, but I could not help it. Every little noise in the shop sounded like a train wreck, and the warm weather smothered me under my annoying long dress. I sweated like a loaf of bread rising under a towel. I wanted nothing more than to go sit in an air conditioned room away from the summer's heat and all the noise, but the only cool place to go was Nina's, our English neighbor. That idle thought died as quickly as it showed up because I would have to sneak over there, which I knew would be unsuccessful.

As I worked, I kept asking myself, *did I do it right last night?* A running argument droned in my brain: *No, you didn't... Yes, you did... No, No... you didn't know any better... why didn't he tell me... you should have... you could have... you were supposed to... you were supposed to... you were supposed to... gah, SHUT UP and relax!* I wished my brain had a shutoff valve or I could win arguments with myself.

The previous night something had taken place which I hoped would never happen. If only people would have opened their mouths and told me what to expect, life would have been so much easier to deal with and I would not have ended up feeling like a fool.

After the singings, three boys approached me and asked if I would be willing to have Abraham for a date. Everyone called him Abe for short. My fear had just become reality. *A guy asked me for a date... so now what?* The thought of riding home in a buggy with Abe made me nervous.

"No, I don't want a date with him," I answered, hoping they would go away and leave me alone.

"You have to do it, this is your first *schnitz* and Abe is the perfect guy for you."

"No, I am not ready yet," I blurted.

"You will never be ready, so you might as well just get it over with right now," one of the guys argued.

I did not know if I should continue to say no, or just accept it. It felt like they had already made up their minds and I did not have a choice. I remained silent for ten minutes and the boys just stood there, waiting for an answer. Since it was dark, I could not see their faces very well, but I knew they were staring at me; it made me uncomfortable.

Finally, the shorter guy with a manly gruff voice broke the silence: "We are not leaving until you say yes."

I gave in. "Ok, I will do it." My head spun as the words tumbled out.

Abe was a tall, handsome guy and was several years older than me. He already had plenty of experience in dating and I felt I was not good enough for him; plus, he was my second cousin. I did not understand why he was still single in the first place. Most people got married by the time they were nineteen or twenty.

Happy with my decision, the boys hurried back to the barn where Abe waited for my answer. The first date is known as a *schnitz,* meaning "first kiss," and here I was going home with the most eligible bachelor. And I had no idea what I was supposed to do. I was sure I was going to mess up somewhere between then and the next morning. Since my first singings experience, Jacob had made no effort to talk to me about what would be expected of me. I felt hopeless because I did not know if the rules even allowed me to ask him. How hard could it be to tell a sister what would be expected? This was not just a simple dinner and movie date, it was a complicated, "figure-it-out-on-your-own" date... . I stood nervously outside with a group of girls and, except for a bit of whispering, they were unusually quiet. It became clear they had no intention of sharing with me what was about to happen.

As I tried to absorb the idea of Abe taking me home, a buggy pulled up close to the house and someone called my name. I could not see anything except the lantern hanging on the side of the buggy. It cast a small yellowish light and threw creepy shadows on the ground. I crossed the grass to the buggy, climbed up, and sat next to Abe. Some of the guys yelled something to us and flashed a light in our eyes as Abe guided the buggy out of the driveway. I was so nervous I had no clue what the boys were yelling.

The ride home passed smoothly, but my stomach flip-flopped like a fish on a riverbank. Abe made it worse by not saying much. After what seemed like an eternity, we finally arrived at my parents' house. Abe climbed down, unhitched the horse, and led him in the barn. I hustled upstairs, threw off my Sunday clothes, and snugged into a navy blue nightdress I had made specifically for this moment. Mem had made sure I knew I needed to make a new nightdress after I started attending the singings. I already had several nightdresses, but the colors had faded. She did not tell me anything else about what I should do to prepare, but the smile on her face told me she was proud her oldest daughter was now old enough to date. She probably thought the singings and the dating would mold me into the young, behaved, church-going lady I was supposed to be. I hoped I would not let her down.

After I had changed into my nightgown, I sat on the bed and waited. Twenty minutes later, I heard Jacob arriving home too. Since he was going steady with Abe's sister, Anna, he had to wait until Saturday nights to have a date with her. He could take her home on Sundays after the singings, but could not stay with her.

Jacob clamored upstairs with Abe and they both came into my room. I scooted back against the wall and listened to the two boys talk. All too soon Jacob left and went to his own room. Abe sat in a chair at the end of the bed and did not say a word for a long time. Because my parents were building a three-story house at the time, we lived in a temporary building which would later become the shop. As a result, my room was partitioned off with plywood and did not even have a proper door, just a piece of cloth hanging in the doorway for a little privacy. After Jacob left the room, a hush spilled over the building, and it got so deathly quiet I could hear my sisters snoring from across the hallway. Right then I would have paid anything to be snoring too, but not with Abe in the room.

Finally, Abe took off his shoes and socks and said, "Well, it's about 1:30, I guess it's time to go to bed."

My mind blanked; I did not know what to say. I laid down right where I was sitting. I wanted to hug the wall but was afraid Abe would think I did not like him. He blew out the oil lamp flame and crawled into bed under the covers. I froze and could not even swallow or breathe. *What is he going to do next?* I thought, panicked. *Is he going to sleep? There is no way I will ever be able to sleep with him laying here.* I did not have time to think long. He turned over and eased his arm under my neck, then he pulled my body up close to his and cradled me four or five times while kissing me on the cheek. Then he slid his arm away and moved a little to the side. I could not speak. If Abe had said anything to me, I did not hear him. He did this same ritual three more times before he quit and fell asleep. I was so tense and scared I did not know what to do with myself. I am sure Abe could tell I was a nervous wreck. I was so confused because I was almost certain he expected me to reciprocate, but I did not know for sure.

At 3:30 in the morning, he woke up, put on his shoes, and left to go home. I had lain awake all night and my head pounded more than my heart. So many thoughts spun through my mind, and most of them told me I would never ever have another date. I would be embarrassed for the rest of my life if I learned I did not do this date right. I lay in bed wide-awake and unable to move for two more hours after he left. Suddenly Mem called my name from the bottom of the stairs—it was time to get up and help with the chores. I sat up wishing what I had just experienced was a nightmare. A bad nightmare.

I dressed and went downstairs to help Mem make breakfast. She did not say a word about someone staying overnight, but I thought I saw a little twinkle in her eye and the tiniest smirk on her face. Her reaction baffled me, and I felt a little hurt. I slammed the dishes around so she would notice I was upset, but she ignored me. Surely my parents heard someone leaving early in the morning, but if they did hear something, they did not let on. I slinked to the basket shop that morning after breakfast, and I felt sick to my stomach. A bad headache pounded the inside of my skull. I wished I could go back to bed, but Mem depended on my help to fill the basket orders. After a long, distracted morning barely holding back my tears, Rhoda called everyone in for lunch.

§

Life went on. Several months passed before another group of guys approached me to match me up with another date. This date turned out even more embarrassing than the first one. To make things worse, my chosen date could not have been farther from the right match for me. His name was Aaron. I had seen him several times but I had never said a word to him. I had no romantic feelings for him at all. He was tall and lanky, with green eyes and blond hair. His facial features made him look older than he really was: he had a wrinkled forehead and sad droopy eyes, with an extra big nose. My guess was he was maybe eighteen years old.

It was not customary for guys and girls to talk to each other outside of church if there was potential they could have a date, so having no previous conversation with someone before being forced to stay together in a tiny bedroom was very difficult, especially when I was not attracted to the guy. Aaron and I sat in my room not uttering a single word, which made it a very awkward night. By then we had just moved into our new house, so I had a proper door for my room and real walls, not just plywood. I could not hear anyone snore anymore, and this only made it quieter.

After more than thirty minutes of absolute silence, Aaron did something very strange: he got up and left. He had already taken off his shoes, but he put them back on, walked out the bedroom door, and hurried down the stairs. At first I was curious as to why he did not say what he planned to do, then I thought maybe he only needed to use the bathroom, which the men could do anywhere. But after ten minutes I heard a horse and buggy crunching down the driveway. Aaron had left! *What a brilliant idea he came up with*, I thought. *No one will ever know we did not actually have a date.* On the next date I would just tell the guy to leave after everyone had gone to bed. I lay down with such a sense of relief I managed to get four hours of sleep before it was time to get up.

The next Sunday in church, though, I noticed the young people laughing and making fun of me because of what Aaron did. I could not understand why leaving was such a bad thing. Why did he tell anyone about it at all? It did not take me long to realize he did it just to embarrass me. I was hurt and angry, not only with him, but with everyone else too. My insecurity level shot through the roof.

§

A month later, my next date turned out better than the previous ones, except, again, the guy was by far not my type. He was known to be mentally off, and he was desperately looking for a girlfriend, which he made quite obvious by his actions. He tried too hard to be flirty—it was not even attractive. His forced smile was not cute either.

It all started one late November Sunday evening after the singing was finished; a couple of guys approached me and wanted me to give permission for Elmer to take me home for a date. I almost fainted. I could not picture myself having a date with this guy. As it turned out, Elmer had indeed said he wanted a date with me. I argued with the guys for a while, telling them they were crazy for trying to set this up.

Nevertheless, I gave in. Standing up for myself never seemed to work, and after all, wasn't I supposed to obey? Elmer was in a good mood that evening and he chitchatted all the way home. It was twelve miles from where the singings took place to my house, and it took a good hour with a horse and buggy. It was the longest buggy ride I ever had. To make matters worse, the night was chilly so we had to cover up with a buggy blanket. Elmer kept tucking his side of the blanket in tighter and tighter. Inch-by-inch my end of the blanket disappeared, leaving me exposed to the clear night air. I realized he was trying to pull it away from me so I would have to sit closer to him to keep warm, but I did not give in to his little game. The more he pulled on the blanket the harder I sat on it. By the time we got to my house, my legs were numb from bracing myself so hard. I jumped off the buggy quickly and wobbled upstairs to my room. I took off my shoes as fast as I could and wiggled my feet to get the blood flowing again.

Elmer went to the barn to put up the horse. Then he came to my room, along with Jacob and some of the neighbor boys who had initially asked me to have a date with Elmer. The guys hung around my room for a while, visiting and joking around. I kept very quiet and sat on the bed with my back against the wall. After a while, they all left, including Elmer, who followed them outside. Jacob waited a little bit by the door until the others were out of hearing distance.

"Don't let Elmer do anything to you," he whispered.

Before I could say anything, he shut the door and hurried down the stairs to catch up with the rest of the guys. I sat on the edge of the bed, completely stunned. Why did Jacob say that? His face looked a little worried, but I did not understand why. I wished I had had a chance to talk to my brother—his warning scared me. I thought if Jacob had any say-so in the matter, he would not have let Elmer have a date with me. I came to find out during my date with Elmer that I had not done what was expected on my date with Abe. My hunch had been right after all. Of course, I had to discover it on my own.

We chatted most of the night and followed the same routine, just like Abe had done. This time I reciprocated. I still felt awkward, and my gut roiled the whole time, but Elmer did not try anything inappropriate.

§

My fourth date turned out to be a disaster as well. I seemed to be a magnet for guys who were not my type, and each time I did not have a choice in the matter. Henry was Aaron's brother. This time I was prepared to keep him in my room, just in case he decided to leave like his brother did. Sure enough, after about two hours in my bed with me, he got up and started to put on his shoes, but I stopped him. There was no way the other guys and girls would make fun of me at church again.

"You can't leave yet," I told him.

Without saying a word he climbed back into bed. I was a little hurt he wanted to leave. For goodness sake, why did he agree to have a date with me if he wanted to leave so soon? Henry soon fell asleep, but I could not sleep and I kept wondering if I had done the right thing by telling him he could not leave. What if he only needed to use the bathroom? If that is what he was going to do, then he probably thought I was a control freak.

The severe headache I had the next day did not make my date worth all the trouble. I wished I had let him go home when he started to leave. I did not know which was worse: telling a guy to stay even when I wished he was a hundred miles away, or letting him go home and opening up the door for people to laugh behind my back again. But if they ever found out I had made him stay they would laugh anyway. Every date seemed to go wrong, each in a new and different way, which made me feel more and more insecure.

I did not want to date any more guys; it just was not worth losing an entire night's sleep over it. However, I did have a crush on one guy for several years, starting when I first saw him at age twelve. Levi was tall and slender, with a good sense of humor and a mischievous attitude. I never said a word to him, but I hoped with all my heart that someday he would ask me for a date. His sisters and I were good friends and we had fun whenever we visited. My wish did not come true, however, and my hopes were crushed when I learned one day he had run away from home. He left the Amish and moved to Nebraska. The only guy in the entire community I wanted to date was now history.

Levi's running away devastated me to the point I could not eat without wanting to throw up. I wanted to leave home worse than ever. I could not help but wonder what would have happened if Levi and I had started dating. Would he have taken me with him? For all I knew I could have been wearing jeans, watching television, driving a car, and wearing lipstick without fear of punishment. Instead, I was still Amish, bound by rules that made no sense, and hating my life. I also thought maybe if we had started dating, we both would have stayed Amish and accepted the rules as they were. Just maybe I would finally have been happy. I did not tell anyone how disappointed I was when Levi left. I even lied to Mem and told her I was coming down with the flu when she asked why I looked so pale and sad.

§

After so many awkward dates and hating every minute of them, I grew even more certain I wanted to leave the Amish. I began to panic because I felt trapped between what I wanted and what the Amish culture required. It was worse when I got sick again, several months after Levi left. This time I did not lie to Mem. I got dizzy very easily and had a weird kind of headache that would not go away. And I began to lose weight. I was scared, not because of my sickness, but because I thought God was punishing me for wanting to leave home. My life was in such turmoil I could not even understand myself. I definitely could not make my parents understand because they would have gone crazy if they knew I wanted to leave.

My parents took me to several different doctors to figure out what was causing my headaches, but to no avail. My suffering continued for a while longer, and I gradually recovered enough to give dating one more try. By then I was seventeen and had determined to figure out a way to be happy without leaving the Amish. I thought if I could find something which made me feel like I belonged, then my Amish life would be so much easier. My only option was to accept the dating rules and maybe steadily date a guy so I could fit in with the rest of the girls who had boyfriends.

My next date was with Norman. In order to give my Amish life one more shot, I was less reluctant toward the guys when they first approached me to ask if I would take Norman for a date. To my surprise, after the date was over and he was getting ready to go home, he asked if he could continue seeing me, and I said yes. I liked Norman—he was handsome, laidback, and quiet. Maybe too quiet, because we did not talk much. He was Abe's brother, so I was dating a second cousin, which I did not care for, but it was common practice among the Amish. I wanted to date Norman because I thought if I had a boyfriend I would fit in and my life would change, but it did not. I only tortured myself more by trying to date someone I liked, but who was someone with whom the chemistry just was not there. It did not matter how handsome he was, it clearly was not working as I had thought. After almost two months, I gave Norman the "glove." "Giving the glove" was an expression used to break up with someone.

As time passed, I got more and more miserable and lonely; I did not know what to do with myself. I desperately tried to find something to make me happy so I could stay with the Amish, but I failed. I was convinced I needed to leave because I was not meant to be Amish anymore. Faking my happiness drained all my energy. I was searching for something I was missing out on, but it seemed to be out of reach. I continued to pray and hope I could find someone to help me get away.

§

It disturbed me that the Amish would let their teenagers have a date in the girl's bedroom, but it was the only way they allowed dating. It had been a tradition for years. There was really nothing else a dating couple could do because they were not allowed to be seen together during the day.

After I started dating, I realized how embarrassing it was when English people wanted to know how the Amish date. No one could understand why parents would let guys go upstairs to their daughter's room to hang out. The main concern people had was about teenagers being intimate, but that was not supposed to happen, and if it did, the couple had to confess it in church privately with the elders.

Our neighbor lady, Nina, gave me her opinion one day while cleaning her house. While I sat at her kitchen table eating a piece of cake, she started asking questions about how many boys I had dated and who they were.

After I told her of several guys, she asked, "Did any of them take you somewhere fun and romantic?"

That puzzled me. I did not know what "romantic" meant, but I had a hunch it had something to do with going out to eat or anything that did not include a bedroom. Nina did not know how Amish dated, and now I had to try to explain it. It was a dreadful conversation, especially since my English sucked.

Nina looked at me with astonishment and said, "That is absolutely wrong and disgusting! How can Amish be strict in so many ways except for the way they date?"

"I don't know, Nina," I answered sheepishly. "It won't do me any good to question the situation, because my parents won't explain it anyway."

"Why not?" she asked.

"We are supposed to be submissive and do as told without questioning anything."

I was relieved when I left her house that day. I did not understand why she thought it was so wrong at the time, but the look on her face made me realize that Amish dating customs really were immoral. In a way, I wished I had not told her about it. I felt bad, but there was nothing I could do to change the rules myself. I could speak out if I wanted change, but, sadly, I knew that talking to elders about any disagreements would be like talking to Minnie the horse.

The older I got the more I realized I had been brainwashed by the whole Amish community and by the ever so "Holy" church. I do not place blame on my parents because they did what they were expected to do. Several months after I had left home, I could still visualize all those rules. One Sunday afternoon I sat outside under a tree and enjoyed the warm breeze blowing through my unfettered hair. I was thrilled I could now wear shorts and a tank top. I could now flush the toilet and not have to wash out the outhouse every six months with a garden hose. I could now drive my own vehicle without fear of punishment; it took me a while to get past that particular fear. I could go to college and get any degree I wanted. I was free to date whomever I wanted instead of being forced to date guys selected for me. I now had freedom most people take for granted.

Even though I was free to date whomever, I realized I was in for a challenge. I did not go on any dates for the first few years because I was extremely shy and I felt like an alien to all guys around me. I was looking forward to going out on fancy restaurant dates, or even going to the beach for a day, but it took me longer than I had expected to get adjusted to my new atmosphere.

Chapter 5:

Silently Angry

Forget how much it hurts and
try again.

~Morely~

As I made my way into the First Baptist Church where I had
been attending for quite a while, I realized how refreshing it
was to have the freedom to worship without the judgment of
others. I could sit down in a pew with red velvet seats in my
favorite pink blouse and black pants, and not worry that I
was not less than worthy of being the true me.

I grew up in a community populated with relatives,
friends, and children of all ages, shapes, and sizes. It was a
community where everyone knew just about all there was to
know about everybody else, and then some. Some of them
were nosey, and others were just plain jealous and
conceited. Despite being surrounded by so many people, I
still felt lonely. I did not feel like I fit in and I wanted to be
by myself rather than hang out with them on Sundays.
When I spent time around them, I felt I had to walk on my
toes so I would not offend anyone. Most of the girls knew I
had been caught with several radios. They also knew what
had happened that one day with Roger. I could tell they

were just waiting for me to make another wrong move so they could gossip behind my back even more.

Roger was not Amish, and looking back on it, I cannot believe I had trusted him. But back then, I had never heard of people hurting someone else.

My bold behavior started when Roger, a sixty-five-year-old man who had become a regular visitor while I sold baskets along the roadside in town, kept asking when he could take me to see a movie. I told him as soon as my parents left home for a few days, when I could sneak out much easier.

After waiting more than six months, an opportunity to sneak out finally presented itself. I took the chance one Thursday night when Mem and my brother Sammie got on a bus to visit Miller Dowdy (my maternal Grandpa) in Ohio. Even though Datt was still at home, I decided to take a huge risk and finally respond to Roger's invitation. So that Friday, while I sold baskets, I told Roger I would finally go. We made plans to meet the next Monday night.

Sarah was with me when I made the plans, and she expressed her doubts about it. The Amish taught that watching television was evil, and Sarah was more concerned about my ending up with a bad illness or a broken leg if the Good Man willed it.

"I know it's scary to think about what could happen," I said, "For goodness sake, I can't even look at the televisions in Wal-Mart without fear of getting a disease." I tried to assure her, but it came out all wrong.

Sarah busted out laughing and said, "I feel the same way when I am at Wal-Mart."

Sarah's confession loosened us both up a little, but when Monday rolled around my level of anxiety and guilt notched up extra high. I wondered why I had made plans to do this when I knew Datt was not going to Ohio with Mem. Not only was watching TV immoral, but driving in a vehicle with Roger, whom my parents did not know well, was even worse. I hardly spoke any English and I figured I would let Roger do all the talking and I would just say "yes" or "no." Sarah suggested I should just stay home.

"I have to do this," I told her. "There is no way to let Roger know I don't want to do it after all. I just hope he doesn't show up."

I was afraid if I did not go out to meet him he would come to the house to look for me. I could not bear the thought of him telling Datt he was taking me to see a movie. Datt would probably have a calf.

The evening rolled around and I was ready to go at 10:30. I waited upstairs in my bedroom until everyone was asleep. Then I crept down the squeaky stairs and made my way outside. I waited a bit at the door to make sure Datt did not wake up. After I was sure no one heard me, I ran down the gravel road barefoot. After a little while, I slowed to a walk. All kinds of scary noises erupted from the dark woods, almost scary enough to make me turn around and run back to the house, but it was not long until Roger came driving up the road in his little green pickup. I climbed in and immediately felt safer. He drove me about 25 miles to his house and we watched the movie *Dances with Wolves*. I was sixteen years old, and that was the first movie I had ever watched. I was scared through the entire movie because of the Indians—they terrified me and I had no idea people like that even existed.

After the movie finished, Roger took me home; it was about three o'clock in the morning. Roger was a nice man and he respected me. He did not try to take advantage of me because we were just good friends, or that is what I presumed. Back then I did not know the dangers of getting kidnapped or raped, or even worse, getting killed. I had never heard of such things happening in an Amish community. I always assumed no one wanted to hurt someone like me if I did not do anything to give them a reason. If I had known then what I know now I would have never gone out like that.

I consider the experience with Roger as a time God wrapped His arms around me, protecting me, and maybe even inspiring me to continue with my plans to leave the Amish. Roger had known I wanted to leave since I was fifteen years old, and we had talked about it all the time. He had given me some pointers on what to expect in the real world, and he had even told me he could give me a place to stay. Of course, when the time came he backed out.

§

My boldness got placed on hold soon after the secret movie night. It was an embarrassing moment in my Amish life, but something I do not regret. It all began one hot August day in 2004, when I was sixteen.

After long hard weeks of weaving baskets by hand, I always looked forward to an occasional day off when we would go to what I called "fantasyland." My parents had found a spot to sell baskets soon after we moved from Ohio to Missouri. The location was perfect because our setup was close to Interstate 35, where many travelers exited to eat at a popular restaurant and truck stop called Dinner Bell. The interstate was in plain sight, and sometimes I would count the vehicles by making a mark on a piece of paper for every vehicle going north and south. It was a great way to pass the time between helping customers. Sometimes Sarah and I would pick out different cars and trucks we wanted to own someday. Then there were days when I would open up the back end of the buggy, sit on the tailgate with my feet hanging down, and take off my white cap to let my hair fall loose and just enjoy the fresh air. I would daydream of the day when I could have my long brunette hair blow in the wind free as a bird forever.

Sarah and I always had a good time when we were together, especially when we sold baskets. We learned how to use a camera so we could take pictures for the many tourists who asked to be in a photo with the horse or the handmade baskets, and if they wanted Sarah and me to be in the photo, we gladly accepted their wishes and posed. Amish rules forbade us from having our picture taken, but some days the rules just did not matter to us.

Sarah and I were selling baskets at the truck stop that day when Roger stopped by to visit. He asked me to go with him to buy cold beverages, thinking it would be a treat for us. I really did not like any kind of pop because I did not like the burning sensation in my mouth from the fizz. Besides, my parents did not really want us to drink pop since it was not good for our health. Instead of telling Roger I did not want a drink, I got into his vehicle. I thought, *What the heck? Riding in his van could do me no harm.* We drove a few blocks to a small gas station and bought Coca Cola while Sarah stayed with the baskets.

When we returned, Roger parked the vehicle and told me I could stay in the passenger seat if I wanted to. He offered Sarah to sit in the back seat to cool off too, but she declined. So I sat there, drinking my Coke and listening to him talk about himself. He was a part-time postal employee who delivered mail from one post office to another every evening, and he did not care whether we understood what he was saying as long as he was talking. I was not paying any attention to my surroundings when Sarah's hollering jolted me out of my daydreams. "Emma! There is a buggy coming up the street!" Sarah yelled in German. "It looks like Mem and Datt!"

"Oh no! I am in serious trouble now!" I shouted. I panicked. My bones froze. I tried to think of a fast way to escape the vehicle without my parents seeing me, but it seemed impossible. I started shaking and Sarah, who stood next to the van, franticly yelled to me to hurry and get out. She looked pale and scared too. There was only one option left: climb out of the vehicle even if my parents saw me. Everything happened so fast it felt like it was just a bad dream. Unfortunately, it was real.

Datt drove to a telephone pole to tie the horse, which was a few hundred feet from where I stood next to Sarah. Roger stayed in his vehicle. Even though Sarah and I could not speak English very well, Roger knew we were in trouble and he tried to keep a conversation going. When we did not respond after a minute, he gave up.

Sarah and I tried hard to act like nothing had happened, but we soon changed our minds when Mem began walking towards us. She had a fuming look on her face, which told me my life would soon be even more miserable than it already was. Datt stayed behind. At first, I was glad he did not get off the buggy because he had a temper worse than Mem, but after seeing her face it did not really matter which parent came forward. She walked over to Roger first and flatly told him to leave. He instantly complied.

Next she spun around and looked at us, "What do you girls think you are doing?"

"Roger asked me if I wanted to sit in his van to cool off and drink a Coke," I answered sheepishly. "I didn't see anything wrong with that."

"He could have taken off with you," she scolded, almost in tears.

I did not say anything, and Sarah stood deathly quiet. I wondered why she did not have anything to say like she always did when we got into trouble. However, I was the only one really in trouble, so I could not blame Sarah for her actions. Or inactions.

It may sound wrong to trust a 65-year-old man to not run off with me, but I had known Roger for over three years. He had stopped almost every Friday just to visit and pass the time. I could not imagine him kidnapping me. If he really wanted to take us, he could have done it a long time ago. It did not occur to me he only stopped when Sarah and I were there, but Mem told us he only stopped occasionally when she sold baskets. I had a feeling Roger did not like Mem, but who could blame him? Mem did not easily warm up to strangers, especially English people.

I decided not tell Mem I had gone to the store with Roger. All my parents saw was me sitting in his van, and I reasoned that if I let them believe I was sitting in the vehicle to cool off, my punishment would be less severe. She did not ask if we went anywhere, so I decided not to bother providing any further details.

Mem broke the silence again: "I wonder what else you girls do here that you shouldn't."

For the first time one little word squeaked out of Sarah's mouth: "Nothing." I kept my mouth shut. And because of my actions that day with Roger, my fantasyland became history.

§

The next six-months dragged by slowly and painfully. All my friends found out because Rhoda told them what I had done. It took many sleepless nights to get over the humiliation of what took place that day because other people now knew about it and judged me harshly. *Where did I go wrong in life?* I would lie awake at night wondering if other girls were as senseless and naïve as I was. Probably not, but we never talked about anything other than well-behaved "lady like" subjects. It bored me out of my skin.

Sarah and I were very close, and it seemed like Mem and Datt tried everything they could after the incident with Roger to not to let us do anything together. I felt bad that my parents were punishing Sarah too, especially since it was my fault. We were so scared of my parents we did not even dare to be together upstairs in my room for fear of Datt sneaking in and discovering us. He would occasionally just walk right into my room without knocking and start looking through my dresser drawers very slowly, his pipe dangling from his mouth. It irritated the crap of me.

Sometimes I could not remember where I had hidden my secret stash of nail polish, lipstick, and a little bit of jewelry. All I could do was sit and hope everything vanished as Datt got close to finding it. Our neighbor lady, Nina, had given the makeup to me once after I cleaned her house. I never wore any of it because the Amish forbade it, but I did not want to part with it either. If Datt ever found out about it, I would have had some hard explaining to do. I could not handle the fear of getting caught with it, so I dug a hole behind the house under a tree and buried my wooden box of possessions. Before I buried it, I locked the box in case someone stumbled across it, then I wrapped it in a plastic bag to keep the moisture out.

The punishment probably seemed harder and more miserable because my parents no longer allowed us to go to the corner to sell baskets. The stress of trying to be on good behavior even affected our daily activities: instead of talking and having fun while cooking and washing dishes three times a day, we did our work in silence, each tending to our own duties in the kitchen. We did not know if we could even look at each other if either Mem or Datt were near. It was miserable. I could not understand at the time why sitting in someone's vehicle could make my parents so angry and ruin my reputation with my friends. More than ever, all I could think about was figuring out a way to run away.

My workload doubled, or maybe I thought so because I felt guilty about my actions and tried to work harder to convince Mem and Datt to appreciate me more. Of course it did not work. I could feel Datt getting more distant from me. We were not close to begin with, so as it became harder to please him, I felt even more unappreciated. Maybe I deserved it, but I also wanted another chance. My whole life I had tried to do things the right way to seek approval, but that was impossible because my parents never affirmed us. So I gave up.

It annoyed me that Datt would not help make baskets more often, and I learned that asking him to help only made him angry. Mem wanted him to at least cut out the wood needed for the baskets, but he did not. He kept busy doing his regular job: sitting around and smoking his pipe. Even after almost losing my little finger while cutting wood with the table saw, he made no effort to take on any more responsibility. After that I was scared to death to continue to using the table saw, but it had to be done to make baskets.

After completing our three-story house, Datt took a break from work and it seemed to last a long time: Following the move to Missouri he did not continue with the sawmill business, and he failed at many attempts to start something on the farm to make an income after that.

On his first attempt to provide for our family, Datt bought beef cattle and allowed them to graze on half of the 125 acres he owned; we raised crops on the other half. The cattle business did not work out too well. Wintertime was rough on the cattle, and it took a lot of hay to keep them fed, which was something Datt did not have plenty of. Then one day he got a wild hair and bought a hundred sheep. The barn and the pasture were not prepared to handle such beasts. Sheep always escaped through the smallest holes, they were always hungry, and they were always loud. When they started to give birth, the ewes lowed so loudly I thought they might as well have been laying eggs. Most of the sheep bore either twins or triplets, but some gave birth to as many as seven babies at once. It was a complete disaster to take care of so many babies: many of them got sick, some lost their mothers, and mothers lost their babies. Datt soon lost interest in them and handed the responsibility of taking care of them over to us.

Next he decided to buy seventy-five rabbits. No one else supported the rabbit business because we all knew he would wind up forcing his children to take care of them, even though he promised he would not. I would pick loud sheep over stinky rabbits any day. Datt penned the rabbits up in a barn, and while they could not get out or make loud noises like the sheep did, they pooped a hundred times a day, and soon the building filled up with manure we had to haul out. The odor from the rabbits and manure grew so severe no one had any interest in taking care of them. For his part, though, Datt kept his promise and did his best to raise the rabbits as much as he could himself.

The farm kept us busy. The boys worked for other Amish people at both a sawmill plant and a metal shop business. The girls worked in the house and helped on the farm from sun up until sun down; there was never any time to relax and enjoy life. Sarah and I finally got used to having a double workload, and our punishment eventually seemed less severe.

§

I believed there was another world out there, if only I knew how to escape this one. I was not looking for just any kind of escape, but I knew there was a destiny beyond my understanding. I knew it would be revealed to me if I persisted.

I thought I had someone to help me make my escape, but that changed when our neighbor lady, Nina, died of a sudden heart attack. I had been cleaning her house for three years, and at one point I confessed to her I wanted to run away from the Amish. I do not think she took me seriously since almost every child goes through a stage where running away sounds like a good idea. However, she said she would help me find a place to stay if I waited until I was eighteen. We did not talk much about it because I was still only fifteen at the time, but I kept my eyes and ears open for any opportunity to learn more about the outside world.

Meanwhile, I planned the escape in my head. The plan included Nina helping me even though I was a little scared of her; I was certain she hated Amish people, but it was probably just in my head. She was not always the friendliest woman towards my family, and her goddess-like personality made me very insecure with the way I lived. And being unable to speak much English did not help my confidence.

After Nina died, I started thinking of other people who could help me. I was not sure about Roger anymore, since I could no longer communicate with him. It took me a while to realize it, but there was one other person, an outsider who had been around the family for a while. I did not think about asking him for help at first because he had a close connection with my parents. That could have spelled disaster because there was no way I wanted them to find out what was on my mind.

I met Virgil one day when he stopped by the farm to chat with my father about horses. After that, he started showing up on a regular basis, and eventually I met his wife Jolene. They were the nicest people I had ever met, and I was flattered they would visit the farm. Virgil had a charming and opinionated personality, which created some tension between him and Datt. Sometimes the questions Virgil asked about the Amish lifestyle made me want to bury myself because I knew Datt did not appreciate an outsider digging for answers he could not explain. Amish would rather just leave questionable actions under the rug and live quietly as they were raised to do. Most of the tension originated from questions asked about church, or Christianity, and education. None of those subjects ever made sense to me. It was complicated.

Despite the embarrassment, I was drawn to Virgil and Jolene because I was curious about the English world more than ever. I needed to hear everything possible, as it gave me hope for my future escape. I did not have enough guts to ask many questions about what it was like to live as they did. All I could do was observe silently. Mem and Datt would have become concerned if I began to ask too many questions.

In late 2004, when I was sixteen, and after Levi had left the Amish and I struggled with the dating scene, I started to get headaches regularly, and had to get some doctoring done. During this time, I finally had to think about giving up my plans to leave the Amish. It felt like I was having bad nightmares, horrible dreams that had been going on for years. Circumstances forced me to plan the escape by myself, and it was taking a toll on my health. I was confused and angry with my life, but I blamed myself for my unhappiness because I thought if I just behaved better, then I would feel better. I had been caught sitting in Roger's vehicle, and Datt had found out I had hidden four radios in my room. I had a nervous breakdown and thought for sure God was finally punishing me, just like I had always expected.

My sickness became worse and I started to throw up and feel very weak. All I wanted to do was sleep; once I fell asleep, it was hard for me to wake up. I cried a lot in my room. The only good thing about being sick was I got a break from dating anyone.

My parents hired Virgil to take me to an Amish lady chiropractor and herb doctor about sixty miles away. She massaged my neck then used a small flashlight and looked into my eyes with a magnifying glass. My datt used to do eye readings when I was younger. Amish people from all over the community and surrounding areas would come to him and let him read their eyes. He had a chart which showed a diagram of everything that could be wrong.

Whatever the chiropractor saw in my eyes must have been serious because she talked to Mem in private about it. Later I found out from Virgil the doctor thought I had a tumor on my brain. I did not realize the seriousness of having a possible tumor, so I did not worry too much about it. I went to the Amish doctor a couple more times before she referred me to a quack doctor who specialized in shooting balloons up the nose. The balloon therapy was designed to help people with headaches by relieving the pressure. Quack doctors were not really doctors, but it was the only thing my parents believed in.

The balloon doctor was in a small town in Lathrop, Missouri, out in the middle of nowhere, about eighty miles away from home. The first time I went to see him, both Mem and Datt came with me. Virgil drove. It was okay to hire a driver to go to the doctor, but beyond that, Amish were not allowed to hire a driver. Horse and buggy was the main transportation. I should have been thrilled to get a chance to ride in a car, but I was too sick to care.

When we got to the doctor's office, I had no idea what to expect. All I knew was he was a quack. After confirming my appointment, I sat down in the waiting room next to Mem. I started to feel paranoid from the small space and the bad, suffocating smell. *Oh Good Man, why in the world am I here?*

An elderly woman came out from the back room, and as she paid her bill I heard her tell the receptionist how much better she felt. I thought to myself *Okay, this can't be too bad then if she likes it.* Soon a tall, long-legged gentleman in a white coat came to the door and called my name. Datt jumped out of his seat and walked to the doctor ahead of me. It annoyed me because the doctor called my name, not his. *What is his hurry?* I wondered. I did not want Mem and Datt to go back there with me. My English vocabulary was worse when my parents were listening, and I could never say what I wanted because they intimidated me.

I greeted the doctor with a forced smile and a handshake.

"How are you feeling today?" he asked.

"Umm, I am feeling fine," I lied. My hands were sweaty and cold.

The doctor smiled and said, "Something tells me not to believe you. Don't be nervous, everything will be all right."

I followed him to a room behind the receptionist and sat down to answer several questions about why I came to see him. Datt could not keep his mouth shut and tried to answer questions for me. This is why I wanted to be with the doctor all by myself. With Datt butting in, I shut down completely. The doctor proceeded to tell me about the method he planned to perform, and he assured me it would not be bad. I wanted say, *Are you kidding me… what you just told me sounds terrible,* but I kept my mouth shut and my thoughts to myself.

Soon after the doctor explained everything, a nurse came into the room and arranged a table for me to lie down on. The table was extremely hard. The nurse then pinned my legs, and another person held my head. Then the doctor placed a special kind of balloon, which looked like a gooey white plastic blob, on a pointed piece of pipe. Attached to the pipe was a hand-held device which pumped air through the pipe to fill the balloon while it was shoved up one of my nostrils. They pushed the balloon so far up my nose I felt when it reached the middle of my forehead. Once they had the balloon in place they began to blow a little more air into it and I thought I was going to die. I could not breathe or scream. I grabbed the doctor's arms but he did not budge when I yanked on him. Everything happened in less than minute, but not fast enough for me. Then they moved to the other nostril. With tears running down my cheeks the doctor had enough pity to let me recover a bit before they did the second side. There is not a word horrible enough to describe how awful that experience actually was.

Once he finished, I left the doctor's office with no feeling; my brain could not comprehend what I had just gone through. Apparently, the balloons were supposed to relieve some pressure from the brain, but for me it only succeeded in building up more pressure of frustration and anger.

Virgil had stayed outside in the car while I was with the doctor, so when we got back to the car, he asked, "How did it go, Emma?"

I smiled politely, and sarcastically said, "Great, I feel better already."

My smile and the tone of my voice did not match my true feelings; Virgil did not let on if he noticed. I was far from feeling better, but I could not tell the truth because I felt I needed to say something that would make Mem and Datt feel like they had accomplished something. After all, they were paying for the treatment and I wanted it to work so their money did not go to waste. On the way home, Datt explained to Virgil the whole scenario performed with the balloons. I could tell Virgil was not too happy with Datt's description because he became unusually quiet. But Datt was too excited to notice. I tried to act as happy as possible in the back seat with Mem, but on the inside I was hurt and angry. I knew I was faking my contentment, but complaining was frowned upon, and having an anger issue was a sin—so I just dealt with it the best I knew how.

As soon as we got home, I went upstairs to my room. I lay down on my bed hoping I could go to sleep, but I started shaking and could not find a place on the bed to relax. I was like a dog, turning around three times before laying down. Except I did it over and over again. I prayed to the Good Man to erase the memory of this day and let me go to sleep.

I went to the same quack doctor four more times after the first visit. Each treatment got worse. At first I did not complain out loud; my parents thought I was getting better because that is what I led them to believe. I thought the sooner I got better the quicker the treatments would end. But the suffering became so unbearable I told them I did not want to continue anymore. I started begging them to try to understand the pain I was going through, but they refused to listen.

I hated it when Datt would brag to other Amish people about the balloon doctor. It was something nobody had ever heard about, so he was proud he was the first one to discover the magic. He made it sound like it was the best thing to cure anything. *How could I let him down?*

Virgil came by the house almost every day just to visit and pass the time. Every time he dropped in, Mem or Datt would tell me to say I am feeling well if he should ask. Virgil despised the balloon treatment, so my parents decided it would be better if I made him think it was working.

On the fifth trip to the doctor, I turned to Mem and said, "Don't make any more appointments after this, I can't handle it anymore."

"Well, you should talk to Datt about it," she answered.

That was the exact answer I expected. I clenched my teeth.

"Talking to Datt will do no good because he is so caught up in his newly-found doctor; he would not understand nor will he care how I feel," I muttered to Mem.

"Maybe just one more time and then we can stop, depending on what the doctor says," she reassured me.

"No, Mem, we are not going to depend on what the doctor says," I retorted. "For goodness sake, he'll have me come for the rest of my life!"

She looked at me sternly, and I knew better than to say another word.

I was angry because I did not know enough English to tell the doctor how I really felt about his abusive treatments, nor was I ever without my parents, which made it much more difficult to communicate my discomfort. The worst part was when Datt answered the questions the doctor asked me, and I knew if I said anything it had to be something my Datt wanted to hear. At one point, I was so mad I wanted to scream at everyone, but I kept it all inside.

There is nothing more frustrating than not being able to express your true feelings. Bottling everything up inside was driving me crazy, but at the same time I had to act like an Amish girl and be submissive and do what the elders thought was best. I knew anger was a waste of space, but for the past two months, instead of the butterflies I normally had fluttering around in my gut in fields of rainbow-flavored stomach acid, I had killer bees buzzing around in an angry swarm.

Several times on the way home after leaving the doctor's office, Virgil and Datt argued about whether or not the balloons were working. One day Virgil suggested I go to a hospital and have an MRI done, but Datt would not even hear of such a thing. They got into a big tiff over it. I was in the back seat with tears running down my cheeks. Mem did not go with us that time, so it was safe for me to cry without anybody seeing it.

When we got home I decided to ask Datt about the MRI. He was in the living room, sitting in his chair, smoking his pipe, and opening mail. My chance to talk to him was now, or forever hold my peace.

"What is wrong with getting an MRI done?" I asked bluntly.

He looked at me and muttered, "Don't get that idea in your head." He threw down a letter he was reading and reclined back in his chair, blowing smoke through his nose.

I was not satisfied so I pressed for more answers.

"But what is so wrong with the idea?" I prodded, hoping for an answer which actually made sense for once.

By now Datt was getting agitated. "It costs too much and the MRI machine is operated with electricity which can cause more health problems." He paused, then added: "I am sure you asked because Virgil brought it up."

From the tone of his voice, I knew better than to say anything more. Besides, he would never consider it because an outsider had made the suggestion.

I sat quietly, thinking about what Datt had said and wondered; *Is an MRI really that bad? Could it be worse than the balloons?* I could not imagine it being more expensive than five trips to the quack doctor, although I did not know how much they had paid for the balloon treatments. I had never been in a hospital except for the day I was born, much less knew what electricity had to do with it, so I just assumed it was really dangerous.

I must have been in tears, because Mem walked into the room and asked, "Are those treatments really that hard on you?"

I could only nod my head. If I said anything now I was going to start crying hysterically. Mem tried to comfort me by telling me that after the next appointment I would not have to go back.

Before my next appointment arrived, I decided to try my best to cancel it without permission from anyone. I wanted to go to the neighbor's house and use the phone, but running over there would be almost impossible without looking suspicious. Plus I did not know how to use a phone. So I did what I knew best and wrote the doctor a note:

Dear Doctor,

Hopefully you receive this in time because I want to cancel the appointment for Thursday morning. I won't be scheduling any new appointments.

Sincerely,

Emma Gingerich

P.S. I can't stand your awful treatments anymore and they are too painful. My Dad might like you, but I don't.

I put the note in an envelope and wrote down the address, then, to my disappointment, I discovered the stamp book was empty. I did not have enough money to buy a full book so I gathered forty cents in change, taped it to the envelope, and stuck it in the mailbox hoping the mailman would take it without a proper stamp. My parents were not at home when I mailed the letter, but I told them about it a couple days later, the day before my appointment. Datt was not too happy, but at least I saved him some money that was going to be wasted anyway.

§

The battle against the headaches continued with a different treatment. I got another checkup at the Amish chiropractor and herb doctor. By then enough time had passed for her to find another experiment for me to try. This time it was at a clinic in Kansas City. This clinic experimented with minerals administered through the veins. I had heard the clinic had just started this method and it was still in the trial stages, but many people were already raving about the results. Of course, my parents climbed on board instantly. Another new journey began. I traveled every Wednesday with a driver to Kansas City to have a needle poked into my arm and a mineral solution injected into my veins. I did not know what it was supposed to do to my body because after each treatment I did not feel any different. It was a waste of time and money, but it was not nearly as rough as the balloon treatment.

One morning I woke up early and could not go back to sleep. My gut told me something was about to change, but I could not put the pieces of the puzzle together. I crawled out of bed and opened the window. A sweet, cool morning breeze blew in as the warm sun climbed up through the trees. *Today is going to be a beautiful day*, I thought. I had to go to Kansas City again for my appointment at the clinic for the sixth time. I was tired of the needles they stuck into my arm, tired of traveling five hours back and forth, tired of Datt always acting like he knew how I felt, and tired of being trapped by my own headaches. I was slowly getting better physically and had started going to church with the family again, but I was still lost. My desire to get away from the Amish seemed like a dream. While I sat on the bed leaning against the windowsill and daydreaming, the flame ignited in my head: *Why couldn't I go by myself with the hired driver to the clinic?* I watched as white fluffy clouds played together in the cyan sky. Suddenly I had a brilliant idea: maybe I could talk to Virgil about my plans if my parents did not go with me.

The night before I had heard Mem say she would not be able to go because there were several bushels of green beans to can. Now all I had to do was convince Datt to stay at home too. I could not take another day of riding in the car with him. He always disagreed with Virgil. No matter how wrong Datt was about any subject, he was always right.

I honestly did not think talking Datt into staying behind would be possible because he enjoyed the rides back and forth. Getting to ride in a car did not happen too often, so this was like a mini vacation to him. I had been longing to talk with Virgil about the idea of my leaving the Amish, but was not sure how to approach him. I needed help and I had a feeling Virgil could give me some ideas. The question was: how was he going to respond to me? I was worried he would not approve and would tell my parents about it. Then

I could just forget about ever leaving. Nevertheless, it was a risk I had to take.

I ran downstairs as soon as I heard Mem in the kitchen preparing breakfast. Now was the perfect time to ask if I could go by myself with Virgil to Kansas City.

"It would mean a lot if he stayed home to help get caught up with work in the basket shop," she said when I asked.

After breakfast, while Datt still sat at the table smoking his pipe, Mem helped me to convince him to stay home. He reluctantly agreed, but not without making a snide comment to me about trying to be bigger than I really was. I did not tell him I planned to not make another appointment. I did not see the point in letting a clinic use me for an experiment. If he went with me, I would not have the opportunity to cancel.

That morning, as I sat in the passenger seat on the way to the clinic, I was nervous. But Virgil had a way of telling stories that helped me calm down, although he was clueless about what I had on my mind.

For me, the glass was not only half empty, I personally needed to brave the extreme conditions to find the water, dig a well, fetch a bucket of it, and try to fill up the glass myself. Therefore, I began to fill the glass after completing another round of minerals. I boldly told the nurse I was not coming back for any more treatments. It felt so good to make the decision on my own. I hoped Datt would thank me later for not spending all of his money on something so useless.

Virgil took me to eat a hamburger, and afterwards, in an attempt to continue filling my glass with wine—I mean, water—I spilled my guts to him.

"Virgil, I want to leave the Amish," I said urgently.

He looked at me startled. His mouth was full so he could not say anything for a minute.

"Do you know what you are getting yourself into?" he finally asked.

I shrugged and did not say anything. The tone of his voice worried me.

After some silence he asked, "Why do you want to leave?"

"There are many reasons why I want to leave," I said calmly. "I am emotionally drained from going to the balloon doctor, and Datt still thinks it was a good idea. I think going to church is pointless. I do not like the dating rituals. I cannot express my opinion about things that are just plain stupid. I am expected to get baptized soon, and I do not want to get married and have a dozen kids. I want to get a better education, and I want to have some freedom."

"Whoa girl, that seems like a lot of reasons," Virgil said with a laugh.

I let out a huge sigh of relief. At least he was laughing; maybe confessing to him was not so bad after all.

"I am sorry that you had to suffer through the balloon treatments," Virgil said with a hint of remorse. "I tried to convince your parents not to take you there after I learned what it was all about, but they didn't listen."

It was all I could do to hold back the tears, but I managed because I did not want an outsider see me cry. It was nice to know someone else was on my side even if the Amish would not listen to him. He was proud of me for standing up for myself and canceling appointments at both clinics.

On the way home, Virgil asked more questions and I answered as best I could. The one thing that hit me hardest was when he suggested I stay home until I was twenty-one.

"I would leave right now if I could, but I decided to wait until I am eighteen," I said evenly. "There is no way I could handle three-and-a-half more years."

"Where are you going when you leave?" he wanted to know. "You can't just live out on the street."

I bit my lip and said, "I don't know yet, it is so difficult to make any plans. Especially since I am a girl, I have very little freedom and I am scared I will get caught."

"Why don't you just tell your parents you want to leave?" he asked.

"They would lock me up," I answered tersely. "Besides, they'll never get over it because it's a sin to live like the outsiders do."

"Well, I would love to help you, but it will ruin my relationship with the Amish. I can't afford to let that happen."

"I don't want you to help me other than just give me some ideas of how in the world I can get out."

"I will have to think about it, Emma. I need to get all of this wrapped around my head. I promised your parents a while back I would tell them if one of their kids said something to me about leaving."

"Oh, Virgil, no! You cannot say a thing. I will be Amish forever if you tell them." I panicked and began to shut down.

"I made a promise to them," he said with a serious expression.

My heart was beating a million times a minute. I had to convince him not tell them, but I struggled for words.

"I think I could convince your parents to let you go," Virgil continued. "I would think they would want their daughter to be happy, so why would they deprive you of that?"

"I am speechless; I don't know what to tell you," I said. Then I added, "If you could understand my language I could explain to you much better why you shouldn't tell them."

He smiled and said, "Just sit tight for a while, I will first just give them little hints about your situation and see how they react."

"If you use my name they will suspect something is going on."

"I will only use you as an example."

"They are smart enough to figure it out, especially since they know I am unhappy."

"Well, it might not be as bad as you think. Just let me handle it," Virgil urged.

I did not say anything more. I was still not sure it would not ruin my opportunity to leave if I ever got that far. My parents did not care about my happiness; they cared about their image as Amish parents. Giving me permission to leave and do what I wanted would get them into serious trouble with the church. I was frustrated because of my language barrier; it kept me from saying what I really wanted to say.

As Virgil drove north on interstate 35, I sat quietly in the passenger seat and daydreamed of what life would be like if I left. I wondered if I would ever be in the driver's seat of my own vehicle. I could not comprehend seeing myself drive, not only because I would probably wreck, but because vehicles were considered very worldly, and it would be a huge sin to have one. I would have to overcome that fear.

I got home feeling a gigantic weight lifted off my shoulders, yet another weight began to form: wondering whether or not Virgil was going to tell my parents about my confession. I had to let it go and hope if they did find out there would still be sanity—and mercy—left in their hearts. I was determined to continue planning my escape until all of my options were exhausted. If only there was an outsider I could live with until I could get on my feet, but who would take on such a responsibility? I ruined my chances with Roger, although I had a feeling it was ruined for a reason. He was not the one who could help me even though he told me multiple times to let him know when I was ready. Surely the Good Man had a plan for me some other way. I thought it would be easy to find a job, but I did not think anyone would hire me because of my Amish background. Then again, I knew almost nothing about the outside world.

§

Things started to get back to normal after I stopped going to the balloon doctor, and I gradually gained my strength back by taking herbal medicine and keeping positive thoughts. I made up my mind I would never complain of a headache again. While I got stronger each day, my head still hurt, and there was no way to ignore it. It was not easy to block the memories of having my head filled with balloons.

Some nights I got up and kept myself awake because the dreams had gotten that bad. I thought it was better to be tired the next day than to fall asleep and have any more nightmares. There were days when I worked in the basket shop, and out of nowhere tears would start flowing down my cheeks. I tried my best not to let Mem or my sisters see me. I would get up and disappear into the outhouse until I got myself under control. There was a small hole in the wall of the outhouse, smaller than my little finger, and I would look through that hole and say to myself, "Someday I will squeeze through this hole and be on the other side of the wall looking in, never to return."

Virgil and I did not have very many chances to talk about my plans after our conversation. Every time he came to the farm to visit with my father, I was sure that any minute serious chaos would break out because Virgil had told them about me, but nothing happened. Weeks and months went by and I worked steadily in the basket shop to keep my mind off things. I had given up depending on Virgil to give me guidance. I was one month away from turning eighteen when my hopes were ignited again. I was out in the barn getting ready to milk cows when Virgil pulled up in his old blue truck and parked close to the area where we stored the feed for the animals.

"Hey, Emma, can you please come help me unload this feed?" he hollered.

I was the only adult out in the barn, but I still found it strange he would ask me to help. So I walked over to his truck and proceeded to grab a bag, but he stopped me.

"You don't have to help me," he said. "I just wanted to give you this phone number, in case you still want to leave home."

He quickly handed me a small piece of paper and I stuck it in my pocket without looking at it.

"Now," Virgil said in a low voice, "I don't know who those people are that agreed to help you, but they used to be Amish, and a relatively new friend gave me the number. I am sorry, but that's all I can help you with because I can't ruin my relationship with the Amish."

"Thank you," I managed to say.

While grabbing for a bag of feed Virgil continued, "I decided not to tell your parents because your Datt didn't keep his promise about something and we got into an argument, but don't worry yourself over it; it's between him and myself."

I remember this day as if it was just yesterday. When Virgil gave me that number I felt very relieved, but it put a lot more weight on my shoulders in a different aspect. I had no inkling when I would be able to sneak away, but before I could stress over it too much my chance came when I was least expecting it. It was the beginning of my path where I fought to make one.

Chapter 6:

Mission in Action

*We must build dikes of courage to hold
back the flood of fear.*

~Martin Luther King, Jr.~

I woke up from a bad dream. I looked at the clock—it had only been an hour since I had gone to bed. How can it be that, within an hour of falling asleep, I was already dreaming of being home for a visit and trying to run away again? In the dream, four weeks had passed since I had gone home to visit, and I was still trying to leave. After dreams like this, I am always relieved when I wake up to find myself in my own bed in my own apartment far from home. To make sure it was only a dream, I got up and snapped on the light switch and looked around. Thank God—I am no longer Amish. I walked into the living room and turned on the television. I have dreamt many times I am trying to get away from the Amish again, and it is always so much more miserable than what happened in real life. I often wonder why I never dream of going back home and being happy instead of returning and wanting to find my way out again. Instead of making me question my decision, I see each nightmare as a sign I have done the right thing by leaving.

§

It was a cold afternoon the day I walked away from the only life I ever knew. That morning, when Mem and Datt said they were going to town about eighteen miles away, my heart skipped a beat. I knew instantly this was my chance to make my escape. My parents could not be at home when my break finally came.

I could not wait to tell Sarah my plans. She was out in the barn milking our two Guernsey cows before breakfast. I decided to wait to tell her until after Mem and Datt were already gone, just to make sure she would not accidentally say something.

Sarah had always stuck with me while I planned my escape. Out of all my brothers and sisters, she was the only one I could pour my heart out to, and she rooted for me. She wanted to leave the Amish too, but we decided I should go by myself first, then come back for her.

Around ten o'clock, I pulled Sarah into the basket shop and cautiously whispered, "Today is the day I am leaving." There was nobody in the shop, but it felt better to whisper.

Sarah looked at me for a few seconds, scared, but she put on her best smile and said, "Go for it, and get ready for me to come too. How are you going to let me know when I can come?"

"I don't know yet, I have to wait and see where I will end up. We also have to wait and see what Mem and Datt's reactions are after they find out I am gone. I don't know if I can write you a letter because Datt is going to want to read everything that comes through the mail."

Sarah said, "Well, we will figure it out somehow. If nothing else I will sneak some letters in the mail for you and let you know if I have a chance to get out."

I started to get nervous because I realized this would be my last conversation with Sarah, my best friend and the only person who understood me, for who knew how long. I knew the next time I saw her nothing would be the same. I would be an English girl and an outcast. I wanted to give Sarah a hug and tell her I loved her, but affection was never expressed in my family; it would have made for a very awkward moment to do it then.

I left Sarah standing in silence and walked into Datt's shop to make a phone call. I had a cell phone given to me by another rebellious teenager in my community. I had been hiding it in my room upstairs. I had never used a cell phone before except to figure out how it worked. I felt more comfortable using the phone in the shop because I could watch out the windows and have a clear view from every direction. I had to make sure no one was going to walk in on me. Even though my parents were not home, I was scared to death. Getting caught with a phone would be a total disaster.

I dialed Roger's number hoping he would answer without being too surprised.

"Hi Roger, this is Emma," I said when he answered. I was so nervous my heart leaped in my throat and I almost forgot to keep breathing.

"What can I do for you, Emma?" he asked.

I quickly explained to him I wanted to leave the Amish and asked if he could pick me up. I had not talked to Roger since I had gotten in trouble sitting in his vehicle, but I was hopeful he would still want to help.

I could not believe my ears when he said, "No, I don't think I can do it. I am a little busy right now."

I wanted to scream *Why?!* But I was just too shocked that now, when I was finally ready to go, he did not want to pick me up. I did not know how to react. For the past three years he had always been supportive, until we lost communication over the past year. I had written a letter to him, but I was not sure he had gotten it.

"Thank you for your time," I politely said. I was hanging up when I heard him ask, "Are you sure you are actually going to do this?"

"I am sure. I know that today is the best chance I will ever have. Don't worry, I can find someone else to come get me."

"Who?" he asked.

"I don't know yet," I lied. I had an idea, but now I was irritated, and for that reason I was not about to tell him. Besides, my next option was a complete stranger, and I did not want to explain this to Roger.

He said, "Well, call me after you make your escape."

"Ok, I will. I better get off the phone now."

After I hung up, I started to panic. I had a feeling Roger was not busy like he said he was. I began to worry that everyone was going to back out when I asked for help to get away. The thought made me nervous. I did not receive this cell phone for nothing; it was supposed to help me run away. I paced the floor for a few minutes, kicking some of Datt's pieces of scrap wood. Finally, I got enough courage to call the other person, but I did not have a good feeling about it.

I dialed the number Virgil gave me several weeks earlier. If I could just push the talk button, I would have it made. With shaking and sweaty hands, I pushed the button.

Ring... Ring... "Hello?"

Pause. "Ehm... my n-name is Emma Gingerich."

"Oh yes, we were expecting a call from you," the woman on the other end of the phone said. "We just didn't think it would be this soon."

I realized I did not have a time figured out for our meeting, but I got myself together and asked, "Would you be able to pick me up today?"

"What time?" the lady asked.

"How about two o'clock?"

"Okay, that sounds good. I'll see you soon then."

Whew... that was easy, I thought as I hung up after telling her where to meet me. I did not know the person I had just called, I did not even know her name, or maybe she did tell me and I was just too nervous to remember, but she graciously agreed to pick me up. I had to walk four miles to the nearest town because I did not know how to give directions to the Amish community over the phone. Plus I wanted to be out of sight so nobody would see who was picking me up. I wanted to be very discreet so my parents could not find me and take me back home. I had heard of several incidences where the parents found their runaway kids and talked them into coming back home. I was determined not to let that happen to me until I was sure I could not make it on my own.

I made my way back to the basket shop where I found Sarah hammering nails into the workbench.

"Sarah? The nails don't go in there, you are wasting them."

Sarah shyly answered, "I know, I just felt like hammering something."

I did not dare say anything else. I knew she was scared, but I did not know how to make her feel better. Besides, I had a knot in my stomach and did not feel like telling her everything was going to be fine when I was not too sure myself.

Finally, after sitting in silence for a while, Sarah asked, "Did you call Roger?"

"Yes, I did, and he told me no."

Sarah looked at me alarmed. "So now what?"

"I called someone else south of Bethany, and a lady agreed to pick me up at two o'clock. I am going to walk to Blythedale and she will meet me at the bank. I will have to leave at 12:30."

Sarah did not say anything. She did not have to; her expression told me what was going through her mind. I was thinking *Oh my gosh, I will miss her so much*. I looked at her beautiful blue eyes, at her blonde hair. She had always been the funny one, cracking jokes and saying the darndest things. If I got into trouble, she was in it too. As we grew older, we both had grown to hate Datt with a passion. We thought he was just too lazy, and many times he pretended to be sick so we would do his work. He started doing this when his kids were old enough to keep up with the farm and bring home the income. Sarah interrupted my thoughts when she told me she was going into the house to get lunch ready.

"I will be there in a minute to help you," I yelled as she ran out the door and looked back just long enough to give me a smile. *At least she is trying to be cheerful*, I thought. I looked around the basket shop, thinking, *What a mess this building has become.* The material we used to make the baskets lay scattered all over the floor, with a path just wide enough to walk from the chair I sat in to the door. I was so tired of making baskets. Mem had become dependent on me to be the main basket-maker, and I thought maybe after I left the business would go to nothing. The thought scared me.

I scrambled up and started to walk to the house. I did not want to think about what was going to happen because I knew I would feel sad for leaving Mem with the workload. I already knew leaving the Amish would completely crush Mem, and that was all I could bear to think about.

After we finished lunch and washed the dishes, I had thirty minutes to get ready. I did not eat much because my nerves were starting to take over my whole body. Sarah talked and laughed as if nothing unusual was about to happen. It warmed my heart to see she was able to act normally so the rest of the kids would not notice something was about to happen.

I climbed the stairs one more time to get my small stash of money I had saved from making little craft projects and selling them at the truck stop. I lingered in my room knowing it would be the last time. I had spent many nights here, crying and praying in secret. It was the only place I could be alone and vent to the walls to make me feel like I was winning.

I took off my white cap and stared at it for a second. "This is the last time I ever hope to see you again," I muttered quietly. I hated when Saturdays came because that meant I had to iron a cap and sit at a table aimlessly putting pleats in the back. I was never successful with it like Rhoda was with hers. The pleats had to be a certain size and the cap had to fit just perfectly to cover up my hair. Satisfied with my last complaint, I put my cap in the bottom drawer. I did not need it—I would wear a scarf instead.

When I left the room, relief flooded over me. I knew in that moment I was doing the right thing. I walked downstairs and into the living room. Sam sat in the lazy chair taking his lunch break before going back to work. Rhoda sat in the living room too, reading a book. I grabbed a pen and paper from a table and wrote a note to my parents in English.

Mom and Dad;

The time has come for me to leave, I am not happy here anymore. I am sorry to do this to you but I need to try a different life. Don't be worried about me, I will be OK.

Emma

I folded the paper and laid it on the table. I then told Sam to make sure Mem and Datt got the note. I turned around and left the room before he could ask anything. He had no clue what I was about to do. Sarah stood in the doorway and heard what I had said to Sam. Her face was red and I could not bring myself to say goodbye to her. Nevertheless, I felt good she knew what I was doing, but at the same time I wondered what kind of pain I was now causing her. Everyone knew Sarah and I were close to each other, so what I was about to do put the weight of my actions on her shoulders.

So at 12:30 in the afternoon, I walked out the door and left forever the only life I had ever known.

§

I made my way across the driveway into the shop and ran out the back door. I sprinted across a roughly-plowed field, the dry chunks of clay making me stumble. I hurried through a barbwire fence and onto the gravel road. As I got to a patch of trees close to the road, I slowed down; I wanted to get as far as possible before someone saw me. It seemed like everything was meant for me to leave this day, at this exact moment. The Bylers, our only Amish neighbor, were not at home. Thank God. I would have had to plan a different route if they had been home because there was no way I could have snuck by their place without them seeing me.

I was about a mile down the road when I heard a horse galloping up behind me. I turned around to see my brother, Sam, sitting tall on the horse's back, breathing hard.

"Where are you going?" he asked.

Oh dear, he is actually worried about me; it looks like he is more scared than I am. I quickly gathered my thoughts and said, "Someone is going to pick me up and I won't tell just yet where I will be at. You shouldn't have bothered to come after me."

"Rhoda wanted me to ask you what you think you're doing. She read the note you left for Mom and Dad," he said, trying to catch his breath.

"I made up my mind that I am going to leave the Amish and there is nothing you can do to convince me otherwise. I have to find a different life — I am not happy at home anymore."

Sam looked at me. "Okay," he finally said. "*Machts gute*, take care." With that he turned around and slowly headed back. I stood and watched him until he was out of sight. I felt sorry for him, because he obviously was very concerned about my decision.

As I continued walking, I couldn't forget Sam's pale face as he rode away, his straw hat pulled down over his

109

brow. I always thought Sam would run away from home before I did. He never discussed anything like that with me, but it could very well have happened because he was so unhappy at home during his first year out of school. He had a bad temper and often got in fights with Datt. But later he got a job at a steel roof shop and he gradually became a happier person.

As I walked it began to sink in that I was really leaving the Amish, and it was not just a nightmare; instead, it was a dream-come-true. I walked for a total of an hour and a half, and I arrived at the pickup spot a little early. I stood outside the bank, watching cars go by and thinking this was so unreal. I hoped I would soon be driving too. I wondered how easy it would be to switch from driving a horse to driving a car. A red Ford pickup slowly rolled by, and the lady driving the truck looked around as if she was unsure of where to go. I had a feeling it was my ride. My heart pounded harder as the lady came back and turned into the bank parking lot. *Yes, this surely has to be the person to pick me up.*

I walked up to her and started talking, and confirmed she was who I thought she was. The woman's name was Kate, and she told me to get in on the passenger side.

"Are you sure you still want to do this?" she asked, looking serious, as I climbed in.

"Yes, I am definitely sure."

"Okay, I just wanted to make sure you know what you're getting yourself into."

As Kate backed out of the parking lot and turned right onto the highway, I felt a strong sense of relief. I had been on this road many times with a horse and buggy, and if everything went okay, the next time I came through town I would be driving a vehicle with four tires and no horse.

When I got to her house, she introduced me to her little family and then she asked if I was ready to change into different clothes. She said, "There are clothes in this bag that you can pick from."

I looked down at my long dress and black lace-up shoes and thought of the many times I wanted to get rid of them. I was tired of sewing dresses and making sure they fit properly so I wouldn't hear complaints from the snobs.

"Yes, I am ready," I answered. I got a pair of jeans and a long-sleeved shirt out of the bag, and then Kate walked with me to the bathroom. To make sure the children wouldn't hear, she whispered, "Are you wearing a bra?"

"Yes, I managed to get one bra," I answered shyly — I wasn't comfortable talking about womanly things.

"I knew Amish women did not wear bras, so I was wondering if you knew how to wear one. Tomorrow we will go shopping for undergarments and other clothes you might need." She smiled as she handed me some towels and demonstrated how the shower worked. Then she showed me a razor and shaving cream and said, "You might want to consider shaving, and in case you don't know, that is deodorant." She pointed to a funny-shaped bottle sitting on the bathroom counter. "If you need anything, I will be in the living room." Still smiling, she closed the door and left me standing in the bathroom, speechless.

I couldn't utter a word to her. This was so overwhelming — I had never taken a shower with faucets and running water. It had always been a metal bathtub sitting in the washroom, and I had to carry water with a bucket. Amish women don't shave, and I began to wonder if it was true about what I had heard about the "English world," that women shaved their legs and underarms. I didn't have facial hair, so what else could this razor and cream be for if it was not to shave my legs? I was really scared to do it.

And then there was the deodorant. *My word. What is this stuff for?* I remembered the one time I found something similar in Jacob's drawer, but he was trying to keep it hidden. I didn't have the nerve to ask him what it was because I didn't want him to know I saw it. I knew anything hidden meant it was private. I always just assumed that since he was dating a girl, it had something to do with her. Now here I was standing in front of the little bottle, not knowing what it could be. I picked it up and read the label and I was able to determine what it was used for.

By the time I processed everything I began to feel pressure in my head. This was a lot of information for me to have to figure out and not make a complete fool out of myself. I turned on the water in the shower then wondered if I was supposed to shave first and then take a shower. This was getting too confusing. *I am not going to shave now, I need some more time to think about it*, I thought.

After the shower, I got my only pair of panties out of my dress pocket. *I am not going to wear the Amish handmade shorts anymore*, I thought. About six months ago I was in town by myself and was in a second-hand store looking around. I wanted to buy some clothes but didn't know how I would get them into the house without my mem seeing them. Then I came across some bras and decided they were small enough to hide. The only problem was, I had no clue what size to get. Finally I just grabbed one, along with a pair of panties, and hoped they would fit. The clerk looked at me strangely when I checked out. I guess she knew that Amish women didn't wear this stuff. After I had gotten my possessions safely home and hidden in my room, I started the process of figuring out how to wear a bra and wondering when the day would come for me to wear it.

I hurriedly put on the jeans and shirt, and brushed my towel-dried hair. This time I would be leaving my hair down; no more fixing it up in a bun and covering it up with a bonnet. *No more boundaries,* I thought as I peeked in the mirror. I looked tired. Being a runaway girl was really exhausting me. I was not sure what to think about my different appearance. I was scared to look in the mirror too much. I felt proud to have gotten this far, but yet I was still stunned from all the different things I had processed so far that day. *Maybe all this will sink in tomorrow.*

I must have been in the bathroom for over an hour, much longer than I had ever been in a bathroom. At home, the outhouse was not a place I wanted to linger for too long.

That night I fell asleep as soon as I hit the bed. I was too exhausted and ecstatic to think much about my family. They seemed to be so far away from my thoughts.

I awoke with the bright morning sun shining in the window. I peeked outside and saw that sometime during the night it had snowed a little, making everything look glistening and clean. The millions of sparkling snow crystals told me that more angels than I could count were there to protect me and to welcome me into the new world. I had slept better than I had in a long time, and now I started to wonder what was going on at home.

I imagined my mem not sleeping at all, her eyes red from crying all night. She probably didn't have enough energy to make breakfast. I had an awful feeling about how she was taking it. Mem worked hard her whole life and always did what she could to keep food on the table. She was not as strict as Datt, but if she got upset about something, it was time to straighten up fast. I could picture my datt, sitting in his usual chair smoking his pipe after interrogating Sarah for information about my whereabouts. Of course, Sarah didn't know exactly where I was, so I wasn't worried that he would find me before I left the area to start my new life. I had warned Sarah that she would be the first to be questioned. While she assured me she could handle the pressure, I began to worry that Dad might lose his temper and hit her if she didn't tell him everything. I knew Sarah would stand her ground and not give him any more information than she had to, and I knew that that could get her in trouble. I closed my eyes and said a prayer for her.

By now I heard noise coming from downstairs and I decided to put my family thoughts behind me and focus on the new day. I could not wait to go shopping — it would feel so good to be dressed in pants and a shirt, and let my long hair get some fresh air. All this sounded like freedom. *I was in a cocoon yesterday*, I thought, *and today I emerged as a butterfly*. This is what freedom felt like. At last.

Chapter 7:

Nothing Can Break Me

*It's amazing how things can change when
you embrace reality.*

~Steve Maraboli~

It is not how high I climb, nor how far I go; the true
measure of me as a person is how far I bounce after a fall,
and whether or not I land on my feet. I believe I landed on
my feet after a very high bounce. I still wonder how I had
the nerve to just walk away from the only life I ever knew.
Had I known a day in advance I was leaving the next day,
would I have had second thoughts and changed my mind?
Possibly. I knew my break was going to happen sooner or
later, but I had expected to know at least a few days in
advance. Nevertheless, the doors had swung wide open
when I woke up that one beautiful morning, and in my mind
I saw a sign that said *Get your butt out of here while you
have the chance.* When I walked away that day, it felt *meant
to be*, yet the future was very unclear. I had years to plan
my future, but I could not plan it because I did not know
what was available to me out in the new world.

I had no idea what was going to happen or where I
would end up, but I found a great and encouraging family to

help me off to a good start. After lying low in Missouri for a little over two weeks, I got word from a cousin who had left the Amish several years before me that my parents were searching for me high and low. I wanted to get as far away as possible before I let them know where I was. It was not long until my new family offered to give me a ride to Texas where they had some acquaintances, Noel and Irma Wiley. It was a coincidence I knew them too. I had met Noel and Irma very briefly in 2005 when they brought horses to our farm for my brothers to break so they could be ridden and used to pull a buggy. Texas was farther away from home than I had ever expected to go, but since I wanted to get away from everything, it turned out to be perfect.

I took the offer and ended up in San Benito, close to South Padre Island and the Mexico border. On our trip we stopped at the Alamo in San Antonio. I was not prepared for what I was about to see and learn while walking through this sacred building. I had no idea people fought and shot each other in real life. It made me dizzy and emotional as I learned about the Texas Revolution. Amish people were not taught any history about wars or about the world in general. History of the modern world was considered irrelevant to our community.

When we made it to the Rio Grande Valley, the Wiley's agreed to give me a place to stay in San Benito. They were still strangers to me, but I knew if I wanted to begin my new life, I would have to take any opportunity God handed to me. I knew my parents were very heartbroken and needing answers, but I waited until I was safely in Texas before I wrote them a letter. I hoped it would comfort them to know I was being taken care of by a family they knew. The ideal situation would have been a face-to-face conversation with my parents before I left for Texas, but I knew Datt would take every opportunity to drag me back home. I could not let that happen.

Soon after I got to San Benito I moved into a small apartment the Wiley's owned. I went to work for their daughter, Laura Jo, cleaning the newly-built houses in their subdivision. Laura Jo became like a mother and best friend to me. She was in her late forties and married to a wonderful man, and they had two grown children. I was convinced God had sent me here for a reason. She loved to introduce me to new things such as food and movies, but the best introduction to my new life happened when she showed me her contact lenses.

I sat in a restaurant eating dinner with Laura Jo and her husband, Bill, when they tried to convince me some people wore contact lenses instead of glasses. I did not know what contacts looked like so Laura Jo proceeded to take hers out. As soon as she removed it, I screamed and jumped out of my chair. I thought she had taken her eyeball out! I had worn glasses since I was thirteen and I had never heard of any alternative; I made a vow then and there I would never wear contacts. In reality, that vow only lasted eight months, and I have been wearing contact lenses ever since.

While I worked for Laura and grew accustomed to my new life, I also busied myself with locating my birth certificate. I had remembered to look in Datt's desk where he kept a large yellow envelope containing everyone's birth cards with little footprints on them, but I did not have my actual birth certificate. I had snuck out my card several months before I had left. I was lucky I got the card because it was my only proof of identity, and I needed it to get my birth certificate from the Ohio hospital where I was born.

Many people assume Amish women do not give birth in a hospital. It really depends on the situation and the mother's condition when the time comes. Some of my siblings were born at home and others were delivered at a hospital.

After I received my birth certificate, the next challenge was to apply for a Social Security number. I was scared to get a number because the Amish did not believe women should have them, but I realized it was important to have an account and a card with my number on it. I remembered hearing Datt talk about numbers the government issued to people in order to track them down. I wondered if this was what he was talking about. I struggled a bit to get the Social Security number because I did not have enough documents to show who I really was. The birth certificate was not enough. The Social Security office told me I needed to get information from my parents and records from where I went to school. Both of those options were not available. Living so close to the Mexico border did not help either. However, after a long six months of patience and determination, I finally received the card in the mail.

Being told I did not have enough identification hit me pretty hard. I started to comprehend how difficult it really was to stop being Amish. It was not just leaving the community; it was actually shedding my Amish identity and finding a new and different one. It took me a while to find my new self. The hardest part was trying to get rid of the mental images and the feeling I still had of wearing Amish clothes.

The Amish are easily targeted because of their simple clothes, which are mandatory for them to wear in an effort to be "plain" and unworldly. It embarrassed me many times to be out in public where "English" people could see me because I felt them staring and heard them making fun of my bonnet and long dress. Young people were the worst. I wanted to walk up to them and tell them I did not want to be dressed like this, that I did not have a choice. I probably would have said it in German, but at least they would have gotten the picture from my frustration. I did not realize the loathed Amish clothes I was required to wear had actually contributed to shaping my self-image. For several years after I left home I felt like everyone could still see me as an Amish girl clothed in a long dark dress and white bonnet. I had a hard time being in public even though I was wearing jeans and a T-shirt. The stares I saw and the laughs I heard when still Amish were riveted into my memory.

I soon learned that, without my Amish clothes, I was more vulnerable than ever. I had no idea my dress and bonnet had been something of a shield, but I began to realize what Virgil meant when he told me there were many people in the world ready to take advantage of someone like me. I did not know what the phrase "taking advantage" actually meant—I learned what it meant the hard way when a Mexican man raped me twice within the first seven months I lived in Texas. He was in his forties with a wife and several children. I knew him because he worked at the same subdivision where I cleaned houses. At the time of the rape, I had moved out of the apartment and into the country with the Wiley's.

The Wiley's had taken a trip to Missouri and Minnesota and left me by myself in their big two-story house. One morning I left the house to water the flowers, and afterwards I took a shower upstairs. It never dawned on me to lock the door when I finished outside. The man let himself in and came upstairs to the bathroom. He scared the living daylights out of me. He grabbed me and carried me to the guest bedroom, and although I kicked and screamed, it made no difference. I do not remember much after he threw me on the bed except that whatever he did to me hurt like hell.

After he left, I crawled back to the bathroom and realized I was bleeding. When I looked in mirror I did not recognize myself because of the shock. My face was red, and my green eyes, now a dark grayish, looked back at me with a dead stare. A long scratch crossed the front of my left shoulder towards my chest. My hair was so messed up I looked homeless. I put on some clothes and went back to my own bed. I stayed in bed all day, not sleeping, not crying, and not moving a muscle. I just remember lying there with my brain flailing in all different directions. I went into a mode of confusion, and I forgot to eat for several days. Somehow, the nighttimes came and went without me noticing.

After several days of hibernating, I got enough strength to go to a math class for my General Education Diploma (GED), at a special school for those trying to better themselves. However, I was so *fer huddled* (confused) I could not sit through the whole class, so I left early. The bad part was, I did not know what had happened to me or if I should tell anyone. I finally began to vent emotions, but only during the night when the painful memories kept me awake. During the day it did not bother me too much as I kept myself busy studying for the GED exam. At the same time I went to the literary center in town three days a week to learn English, and in my free time I worked on a ranch for a lady who raised riding horses. I had quit working for

Laura Jo because there was not enough work anymore, which I was glad about because I did not want to encounter a run-in with the same man who hurt me.

Even though I kept myself busy, I still felt so disgustingly dirty that I could not take enough baths a day to make me feel clean again. I did not tell anyone about it, and I made the decision just keep it to myself because, after all, that is what I had been taught at home. I was so used to not being allowed to talk about things which did not make sense that I believed what this guy did to me was something girls had to give into.

At the time of the rape, I did not even know what it was called. I did not know anything about sex, which made the horrific experience even more difficult to explain to anyone, even if I had wanted to. I blame the Amish for not educating me about sex. My parents never said a word about it, and I was secluded enough that I did not even think of asking. I always thought it was weird when girls were not allowed to be near the barn at certain times, and later I figured out it was because animals were breeding and our parents kept us from learning about it. I think if I had known about sex and was taught how men were to properly treat a lady, I could have prevented the rape, especially when it happened the second time.

A little over a week later, the same man came back. This time it was in the late afternoon and, of course, I was oblivious to the fact he would return. I just assumed he knew how much he had hurt me the first time, so why would he do it a second time? I was outside in the yard playing with the Wiley's horses. Before I knew it, he appeared right in front of me. I did not hear a vehicle or see anyone coming until it was too late. My body froze the moment I saw him. Paralyzed from fright, I could not run away and I could not scream or breathe. I knew the minute he grabbed my arm and pulled me toward the house that fighting him was not worth it. He was a two-hundred-pound bully with big muscles, and I was a hundred-pound little naïve Amish girl who did not know how to fight or stand up for myself.

§

I recovered faster the second time, mainly because I was determined not to let the dreams I had for the future fail. I did not want to go back home to Amish land, but I knew if I did not keep myself together that is exactly what would happen. I had to stay strong and keep moving ahead, but the painful experiences weighed heavily on my mind. Every day I struggled to put on a smile around other people, but I did it anyway.

A few weeks later, as I searched for some kind of explanation for what had happened, I saw a television news story about a guy who was sentenced to jail for raping and sexually assaulting a girl. My gut told me I had gone through the same thing. By that time I had learned how to use Google on the internet, so I did a search about rape. Suddenly everything fell into place. I learned about rape, incest, committing suicide, and murders. My brain could not comprehend all the foreign stuff I was learning. I had a dictionary with me to look up any words I did not understand, and even then I only understood the gist of it. I did enough digging on the internet until I accidently stumbled across some disturbing information about a few different Amish people, including my grandfather. I was never close to either of my grandfathers, and after I saw what one of them did, my stomach really turned. Another Ex-Amish person, whom I did not know, had put the information on the internet.

The Amish church takes punishment into their own hands, subjecting the offender to a six-week shunning process. After that, the offender has the option to ask for forgiveness, then everything goes back to normal. They get away with criminal acts for which they would serve ten to twenty years in prison in the English world.

The Amish would rather suffer abuse and insult than be involved in any kind of justice system. The Amish consider the criminal justice system too "worldly," and a person can be shunned if they used it for their own good.

I knew who the guy was that raped me, and I was scared of him doing it again if I did not stop it. However, it was hard. I could have told Laura Jo or the Wiley's after they came home from their three-week-long trip, but I could not bring myself to do it. I was not sure how to bring up the conversation, and I was scared that I would be sent back home. I worried that I was becoming a huge pain in the Wiley's lives.

Several months passed and I became so distraught and dysfunctional I could not eat or sleep. People around me noticed something was wrong and they began pressuring me to open up. Finally I could not hold it in any longer and I began to talk about it early one morning after another long sleepless night. I was so tired of bottling things up and I knew I had to do something before I lost any more weight.

Action was taken immediately and the police arrested the guy. The Wiley's drove me to the police station where I pressed charges against him. I had no clue what I was doing, but I had plenty of people helping me get through it.

The court later sentenced him to three years in jail. After he served his time he was deported back to Mexico.

After the rape, I remembered my brother Jacob's words: "Don't let Elmer do anything to you." More than a year later my questions about what he meant that night were finally answered. I realized Jacob had wanted to protect me, but if he really thought something bad could happen, why did he not educate me? I will never know. I had done some unforgivable things in the Amish eyes while at home, and never once did it occur to me that anything bad could actually happen. I had been lucky.

Immediately after the arrest, I felt I could move on. However, law enforcement and other people urged me to go to counseling even though I thought I was doing okay. I took their advice and went once. I stared blankly at the lady who asked me questions about the rape. I got up and walked out of her office before time was up without answering any questions. I could not open up to a complete stranger. I realized every challenge that came my way presented an opportunity for me to grow stronger, and I did not need counseling. I felt much safer and I did not see a point in crying about it any longer. Besides, I was busy taking classes for my GED. I was also more concerned about making amends with my family and trying to heal the rift my rejection of the Amish lifestyle had rent in our relationship, so more than ever I wanted to forget about the rape.

§

In the fall of 2006, after I put the rape behind me for good, I got a job at Dollar General and continued to study for the GED exam. I felt I was now experiencing the real world at its best; I had become one of those women who had a job and was doing something important with my life without having to answer to anyone.

Eight months later, I passed the GED exam on the very first try, within the first year after leaving home. I immediately applied to go to college. Passing the GED was a major accomplishment because the schooling I had received from the Amish was nothing compared to that of the English world.

I had attended a one-room Amish schoolhouse in Missouri where teachers with an education no higher than the students themselves taught first through eighth grade. We studied basic math, spelling, reading, and writing. Spelling and reading were taught in both English and German. For writing, we only had to write sentences using an English word the teacher assigned us to use in each sentence. We did not write any essays. Even though the Amish teachers taught English, we never used it outside of the school setting, except when communicating with English-speaking Americans. We all spoke German in our daily conversations.

When I was still in school, I did not give much thought about my education until I had completed eighth grade and had started working at home full time; then I began to feel a void in my life. For the Amish, education had no meaning after eighth grade. No one talked about or planned a career path. My life's path had already been pre-planned long before my birth: tradition expected me to stay home and work for my parents until I turned twenty-one, then I could start making my own money and do what I wanted. The Amish lifestyle, however, did not offer many options other than being a nanny or schoolteacher, and neither required an education past eighth grade. Everything I knew and did was based on what I learned at home growing up. The fact we were even required to go to school for eight years of our lives still amazes me.

During my Amish experience, I felt something was missing, and even while still living in Missouri I began to realize there was so much more to learn. My pre-planned adulthood did not stand a chance with me. Of course, I could not tell my parents how I felt about wanting to learn more because they would see me as a disgrace to the Amish society. The day I escaped, I did not have a set plan on what kind of education I wanted to pursue, but one thing remained clear in my mind: I wanted to go to college. There were so many things I needed to learn before I could make a decision on a particular career.

If the Amish would consider education farther beyond fourteen years old maybe the people who decide to leave would have more of a grasp of where to begin in a college or career setting. Part of the reason for not offering more schooling was so no one would realize there was more choices in life with an education. As for me, I was clueless what path I would take, but also ready to blaze a path where none existed.

§

When I started working at the Dollar General, I began to grasp what it was really like to live in the outside world. Of course, I was still as naïve as ever, but as the days passed I could feel an inner strength flowing from me. My manager patiently taught me how to use the cash register. I was amazed at how easy it was to use, but I was even more amazed at how easy it was to make a huge mistake and then have to get the manager to untangle it.

Some customers were rude, some were hostile, some were friendly, and then a few were gentle and loving. These kind people would give me tips in five-dollar bills and tell me to buy something nice with it. I did not think I needed anything nice, so I would stick those bills in a donation jar for the Literacy Center. I wanted to help others more than I wanted to help myself, even though I did not have anything to call my own. I even gave a co-worker money every time she complained of not having diapers for her child, or gas in the car to get to work. I handed out cash freely; there was no way I could say no to anyone.

I enjoyed working in this simple little store, but the wrong people must have noticed my naivety, soft heart, and gentleness because someone stole the old 1988 Chevrolet truck I was driving at the time right out of the store's parking lot. I had the keys in my possession, but I must not have locked the doors. My purse with all my money, my Social Security card, my driver's license, and my favorite lip-gloss was in the truck, and was now history. *Why would anyone on this planet earth steal?* I thought. I could not fathom the reality. I cried bitter tears while giving a report to the police. No one had told me not to carry the Social Security card with me. No one had told me to always lock the doors, and no one had warned me that old vehicles could start without the key in the ignition. Even after the rape, I still did not seem to understand how cruel the world could be.

The police never found the truck. They said it had most likely been taken across the border to Mexico and nothing could be done about it. I re-applied for my Social Security card and my driver's license, and then I bought my own vehicle—a maroon Dodge pick-up truck—and continued on with my life. Slowly but very surely I learned how to stand on my own two feet. I let my heart get a little harder, I quit giving money to just anyone who asked, and I fumed over a supervisor who depended on me to do his work.

The supervisor, Keith, was just about as lazy as anyone could get, but it did not bother me until my boss asked me why I was not able to keep up the store. Keith would sit outside the back door with his cell phone stuck to his ear and a cigarette dangling from his mouth for hours at a time. I realized he was just there for the money, and to me he looked like a hoodlum. I nicknamed him Grizzly Bear. He stunk like stale cigarette smoke and old sweat, his hair needed cutting, and his facial hair needed to be trimmed. I often told him he was starting to look Amish, but he did not find my comment amusing. Every time the store got hectic, I had to go on a hunt for the Grizzly Bear. Customers would look at me with a hint of impatience in their eyes if I was too busy to help them right away. This humiliated me.

Not only did Keith not help much with customers, he expected me to do his part of merchandise stocking as well as keep the store clean. After six month of his nonsense, I decided I did not have to be treated this way anymore, so, full-force, I spilled the news to the boss. I blubbered like a baby. I spewed out all my frustrations about the Grizzly Bear in my thick German accent, and afterwards I just knew he was going to fire me for having an emotional outburst. Luckily I did not get fired, but a few months later, Keith did.

I only stayed a month longer because I got accepted into college and I needed to now focus on school.

§

In the summer of 2007 I got my acceptance letter to attend Texas State Technical College in Harlingen, where I lived at the time. I signed up for classes for the fall semester. In order to pay for the classes, I filled out a Federal Student Aid application. Additionally, I had to provide four letters of recommendation because I did not have any of the required information from my parents. One was a personal letter from me, in which I had to explain my background, my plans for the future, and why my parents were not supporting me. I needed to provide those letters to get a financial aid override, so I did not need to have my parents' income tax information. Actually, I did not know if they even paid income tax, but I knew it was pointless to ask because there was no way they would give me that information. In addition to applying for financial aid, I applied for scholarships and grants, and ended up getting enough aid to pay for all my classes and to live comfortably for a whole year. I was amazed at how things fell into place without having to worry myself to death.

I went to my first day of classes; saying that I was nervous is definitely an understatement. I felt like I was an inch tall in a foreign country. I had studied for my GED at my own pace, and did most of my studying in a Literacy Center, so when I started college I had no clue what I was in for. Talk about drinking from a fire hose!

I had no idea what homework was, or even worse, I did not know what quizzes were. Pop quizzes? Never heard of such a thing. Ask questions? No way! I would rather have died than to ask the teacher a question about something I did not understand. I knew if I started talking I would have to explain where I came from because of my bad English

Runaway Amish Girl

vocabulary and thick German accent. I did not want anyone to know I used to be Amish. Instead, I would go home and bust my brains out trying to figure out whether or not I was doing my homework right, and I would attempt to remember the important information I had to know for the next class period. I was all alone in my journey—no fellow ex-Amish people lived in my area to lean on for support, and the few people I did have in my life who I could trust could not understand how I felt. I was scared but excited to find out what I had gotten myself into.

Chapter 8:

A Change of Heart

*Sometimes your only transportation is
a leap of faith.*

~Margaret Shepard~

While I sat in the recliner in my new home in Harlingen
writing a letter to my mem, I wondered what I would be
doing if I had stayed Amish. Before my escape, I had
thought long and hard about what I wanted to do if I had
remained Amish. I knew for sure I did not want to work for
another Amish family again. I did not want to make baskets
anymore. I did not want to be a schoolteacher. I did not
want to get baptized, get married, and have children. Amish
girls did not have much say in how they lived life back
home. If I had stayed, I most likely would have been stuck
at home the rest of my life raising children and doing
housework. Ugh!

Six months after I moved to Texas, I made plans to
travel back home to visit for the first time since leaving. I
felt more nervous about going back and facing everyone
than the day I actually made the escape. I had received
many letters during the last six months, and I feared the first
visit would not be easy. I did not really expect it to be. I

knew I needed to go back and try to explain why I had left rather than just write letters. Running away was not easy, but it would have been much easier if I could have just told my parents I was going to leave. It was very possible I would have been punished, though, for even talking about such behavior. I could not speak to them about anything that bothered me about the Amish rules, so informing my parents I planned to go "high" was out of reach. Being "high" was the phrase used when someone left the Amish. I had tried to give them hints I was not happy, but they either did not catch on or they did not care.

Some of the letters I received before my first visit home confused me. One letter Jacob wrote said, "If you don't make arrangements to stay at home then you shouldn't even bother to come at all."

His statement hurt me, but I thought surely he could not be serious. The only way to find out was to take another leap of faith.

Mem told me in another letter, "You have to wear Amish clothes because no one wants to see you with 'English' clothes when you come home to visit."

As I sat in the recliner finishing my letter, I thought about the dress I wore the day I left. It hung in the closet and I was not about to put it back on to go home. I knew Sarah and Amanda would not mind seeing me in jeans, or at least I hoped they would not.

The Amish believed the Bible condemns those who do not honor their parents. I knew I had disobeyed my parents, but I also disobeyed them at home. I could not see the difference whether I stayed or not. Either way, according to the Amish, I stood condemned.

After I was through re-reading the letter to my mem and reminiscing about the Amish way of condemning me, I continued to build up my courage to take that leap of faith and go visit.

§

My first visit home included my first plane ride to Kansas City. I could not help but feel vindicated that I was able to break another Amish rule—they believed in staying on the ground for any transportation. Slow, stinky horse poop kind of transportation at that. I got horribly sick on that flight, but it was still worth it.

Virgil picked me up from the airport and we drove to his house in Jamesport, Missouri where I met Enos, my cousin who left the Amish shortly after I did. Enos then took me to my parents' house about sixty miles away and dropped me off. I was scared not to have a getaway vehicle in case I needed it, but I rested assured that Enos was only a phone call away.

After Enos dropped me off on that hot June day in 2006, I timidly walked to the front porch of the house where my young siblings sat and stared a hole in me. I did not see Mem or Datt, but I had a feeling they were hiding behind the windows in the house. Even the older siblings were nowhere to be seen. The farm seemed to be deserted. I sat down on the porch with my back turned against the door, not sure if I was welcome to go inside. I was almost in tears when Sarah and Amanda finally slipped outside to join me. I was relieved.

I eventually made it inside where I faced Datt and Mem. Datt sat in his usual chair smoking his pipe; his face was white and his solemn blue eyes darted away from me as he said, "*Vegates*" (Hello).

Mem sat in her rocking chair, her eyes red from crying. She managed to ask in a shaky voice, "*Vee bischt du?*" (How are you?)

"I am doing good," I replied softly.

I sat meekly in a chair in the living room not knowing how to begin a conversation. The little girls followed me in the house and kept staring and occasionally grinning. Mem did not say much, but Datt got impatient and started stirring the pot.

"You look like the world and you live like the world; how can you expect to be right with God?" he asked harshly.

"I don't think God judges me based on how I look, but rather what is in my heart," I retorted.

"And what exactly is in your heart?" He asked so sternly I was sure he thought I did not have a heart.

"I am at ease with what I am doing now. I know that God is watching over me and I am trying to follow the path that he has chosen for me."

Not any calmer than before, Datt replied, "You are going the wrong way and you cannot convince me otherwise. You've been brainwashed and it's scary."

I listened to him for a while longer. Sometimes I tried to put in my two cents, but it did not do any good. No matter what I said, I was always wrong. Datt made sure I knew I had committed a major sin and I was certainly going to hell. I used to think of myself as confined in a little cave. I would peek out a bit now and then and peer around like a mouse huddling in the shadows and looking at the big scary world outside. Deep down I knew if I stepped outside the cave I would speed down the highway to hell. I left the cave anyway, and soon after decided I was not heading to hell for leaving my family. However, it was not so easy for my parents to understand.

After a while, I left the room when there was a pause long enough to leave politely. My sisters followed me to the kitchen and they offered me a glass of water. I did not want to get mad on my first visit home, especially since Mem and my sisters had asked me to stay for the night. I wanted to keep the peace for their sake. With coaxing from Mem, I gave in and put on my Amish clothes. She gave me an ultimatum: either change clothes or sleep somewhere else. I was almost certain Datt had told her what to say to me before my arrival. I thought about it for a minute then decided I would do it out of respect, even though wearing a dress and head covering gave me dreaded flashbacks.

It was worth it that night, though, when I got to spend some time with my sisters upstairs in my old bedroom. They were all a little unsure of how to talk to me, and they never asked what it was like living in the English world. I figured the reason they were not inquisitive was because they just could not comprehend I was now one of the outsiders. The saddest part was noticing the scared looks on some of my siblings' faces. We ended the evening by just having good ol' conversations about their lives in general, like school, work, and who was dating whom. Having conversations familiar to them seemed to break the ice and made it less stressful on everyone.

The next morning, after breakfast, I helped wash the dishes, then afterward my siblings left me alone with Datt and Mem. We quietly sat in the basket shop when Mem finally asked, "What have we done to you that made you leave us?"

I responded calmly: "I didn't have a life here. All I did was make baskets or work for other families. But the biggest reason of all was the fear of having to join the church and then have the pressure to get married. The final decision to leave came after having balloons shot up my nose. It was enough to make any person want to get away from everything."

Datt said, "You didn't have to get married."

"Then why did I have to date guys who were not even close to being my type. I remember how happy Mem was when she found out I was dating Norman and I could tell the sadness too, when I broke it off with him."

Datt soon wanted to change the subject. "I thought you were mad at us for taking you to the balloon doctor and that was the only reason you left."

"I was mad and it was ultimately the final trigger for me amongst all the other things that I didn't like or could not understand. There are days where I still cry when I think about those awful treatments, and to think it was just a nervous breakdown I was going through."

Tears rolled down Mem's cheeks. "I am so sorry we took you to that doctor," she said. "If I had it all over to do again, I would change it."

"I accept your apology, Mem," I replied, choking back tears.

Datt looked at her and said, "I don't think that the balloon doctor had anything to do with it. Emma is just being stubborn and wants to put the guilt on us."

"I can't believe you just said that, Datt," I chimed in. I could not stop the tears now.

I was so furious with his comment I stood up and left the room before I started throwing things in his face. At that moment I realized he would never apologize for taking me to the balloon doctor. I walked from the shop to the house, and soon Mem followed. We sat in the living room and had a general conversation about everyday Amish life. No one brought up the dreadful conversation in the basket shop again.

I stayed at the farm for three days without talking with Datt again. He just sat around the house silently, looking distraught. I felt sorry for him. I could tell it took a stressful toll on him when I left. In a way, I blamed his stress on himself, but I knew the Church and the whole community did not make it easy on him. I could just see a mental image of everyone judging him for the way he raised his daughter.

When the time came for me to leave for Texas again, I was glad. I was more than ready to shed my Amish clothes and change back into something more comfortable—pants and a bright-colored shirt.

A year later, in August of 2007, I visited home again, and this time things went downhill between Datt and me even worse than the first visit. He brought up the same conversation about everything I had done and was now doing wrong, and he preached on and on. I stood up for myself several times, which only made him angrier. Finally, I could not handle it anymore and I started crying and screaming uncontrollably. However, after the first day, everything calmed down again and Datt fell completely silent, just like he did during my first visit.

I changed into my Amish clothes like before and stayed for several nights. I enjoyed visiting with the girls and Mem, except I had to be cautious what I said or did so I would not offend anyone. Everyone was very sensitive. And so was I. I tried to explain to them that I was going to be starting college soon after I got back to Texas. But that information rolled right over their noggins. In the letters I wrote to them I often mentioned the things I was doing, like studying for the GED exam and working at a Dollar General, but they never mentioned or asked me about it. Our conversations mostly stayed within their comfort zone: Amish life.

The next year, in early 2008, after the third visit ended, I vowed to never go back home again. Every single time I visited, I stressed out so much that I almost broke out in shingles. Or it felt like I did. But I had to eat my words when I received an invitation to my brother Jacob's wedding. I struggled with understanding why Jacob invited me when Datt still would not talk to me, but I decided to use the opportunity to show my family I still loved them. I just had to get past Datt's rejection.

§

The letters started arriving a couple weeks before Jacob's wedding, which happened to be scheduled during a busy semester at college for me. I still wondered why he would even invite me. Was it to make me feel guilty? If I did not go, he could make me out to be the bad sister, and if I did attend, he could make me feel uncomfortable and out of place. Either way, I lost. I did not know if he had invited me because he really wanted me to be there, or if his intention was to make me feel bad. I assumed the latter. I did not really want to go because I knew I would have to be Amish for a couple days, and I was not sure I was ready to handle it again after my last visit had caused so many nightmares.

Jacob, the oldest child in our family, was eleven months older than me. He was a quiet man, but I was proud to have an older brother who was handsome and smart and handled himself with humility, like every Amish person was taught. His popularity helped me feel important on those Sunday mornings I rode with him to church.

Although we did not talk about anything serious on those mornings, he could make me laugh with unexpected remarks about nothing in particular. He never opened up about what was going on in his life, and it did not seem right for me to ask him to share anything. He seemed to have his life together all the time, and I envied him. I cannot remember getting into a serious fight with him, and he was not the type to hurt any of his sisters, but there were days he would express some anger towards us if we did not listen to him.

After I left the Amish, though, Jacob surprised me by trying to convince me to go back home by writing a letter designed to scare me. One night, while I was trying to go to sleep, I kept thinking about my brother and his upcoming wedding. I missed him dearly, but how could I summon the courage to go? I looked at the clock for the hundredth time, and at 1:30 A.M. I sat up in bed and turned on the light. I was annoyed with myself and I had no idea what to do to calm down.

Finally, I climbed out of bed, walked to the closet, and pulled out a box of letters. Maybe reading some of Jacob's old letters would help me decide whether to attend the wedding. I found some of them buried under hundreds of others I had received over the past two-and-a-half years. I had mixed emotions about reading them again. I could not remember exactly what he had written, but his letter was one of the first I had received after escaping. I had seen Jacob a few times since, and while it was not easy for him, he had started to accept me the way I was, albeit slowly. I sat on the bedroom floor, my back against the wall, and removed three roughly-handwritten pages, scripted mostly in English mixed with a few German words.

Hello Sister,

Feb. 26, 06

Greetings as always are being sent sadly from me to you. This is Sunday afternoon; I am trying to entertain myself, which is hard to do since you left. I decided to write a few lines your way to let you know what's going on and what is going to happen. I just thought I would try and help you out of your nest that is getting deeper. God up above will hear and see everything you did and do. He will not forget at the end of the world or the end of your life. It is still time to make things right. It will make it much easier for you to face everyone if you give yourself up and come back home. You left a lot of good friends and relatives behind. I can't see how you can enjoy yourself knowing you won't get to see our aunts and uncles and a lot of cousins anymore.

I am thinking you should straighten up because someone once told me that we can't change parents, we just have to give ourselves up first. And I agree, because when I was younger, I had the same feelings you had. Then I gave myself up, Datt didn't bother me anymore and all of a sudden I was happy all over again.

You might be happy now, but think of the time when you are about to die and no relatives to visit with you. Do you think you would be wishing you had listened to Mem and Datt??? I am sure then, that you will cry many nights wishing to be Amish with your brothers and sisters, if not, let me know why? You are crazy for letting yourself go.

If any of your brothers and sisters ever get married wouldn't it shame you to not be at the weddings? And if you did come, do you think you could enjoy yourself as good because you are not Amish? Think about it!!

You might be thinking freedom now, but think of the years ahead. You are the one that is making it hard for yourself and I am here trying to help. I hope you have enough sense to let yourself be helped. Datt is happy to know that you are safe and he wants you to be happy, but not the life you are in now.

How would you like to go to the war? You might not like it, and there won't be a way out of it if you stay English. The computer chips are the same way and there won't be a way to help you out of it. Now I want you to read this a couple times and think about everything hard.

Let me know when you are coming and what you got in mind.

Your brother,

Jacob

Tears erupted halfway through reading the letter. I was not crying because I thought Jacob was right, but because I felt sorry for everyone I had hurt. *Dear God,* I prayed, *please help my family understand why I had to leave them. Amen.*

Jacob obviously worried about what could happen to me. I do not know where he got the idea about the computer chips, and he thought I would end up going to war because I had a Social Security number. Mem expressed the same concerns in her first letter. These comments did not intimidate me because I was confident it would not happen. Either Jacob did not know any better, or he said it to scare me. I was doing what made me happy, and all the angels in heaven had my back. I had no doubt God was protecting me.

Since leaving the Amish I had developed a very different outlook in my faith, and I went to church every Sunday. Going to a church where the preacher spoke English was a whole different learning experience—I had lots of catching up to do! I knew nothing about the Bible. Nothing. Not even a verse a three-year old knew by heart. It took me two years after leaving the Amish to accept Jesus as my Savior, and I even got dunked in a full-immersion water baptism by a Baptist preacher in Harlingen. I always knew the Good Man stood by my side, guiding me in troubled times even when I did not want to believe it.

Reading Jacob's letter again finally brought to light how sad I had made my family. I tried to imagine the pain on Mem's face when she went to church the first few times. She could not hide the fact I was not there, and people probably questioned her inability to keep her daughter at home. If only they could understand leaving them had not been easy on me either, but explaining it proved to be difficult. Homesickness had been beyond hard to describe on some days, but I managed to stay busy to alleviate some of the pain.

I folded Jacob's letter and slid it back into the envelope. A sense of relief came over me and I finally crawled back into bed and fell asleep instantly.

§

I woke up the next morning startled to see I had just enough time to throw on some clothes and head to my 8:00 biology class. Missing coffee and breakfast was not a good way to start my day. I sat in class with my thoughts nowhere near the subject of the plasma membrane of a plant. Jacob's wedding invitation still weighed heavily on my mind, and I remembered the last time I had gone home to visit, my third visit in the spring of 2008.

I vividly remembered driving up the gravel road and turning into the driveway. I was amazed to see Datt was the only one outside, and it looked like he had been waiting for several hours. I found it a little strange no one else came out to greet me, but like the first few times I had returned home, the kids were not allowed to act as if they were glad to see me, so I figured they had been told to stay in the house again.

Datt walked toward the vehicle, and as I opened the door of my Dodge pickup and stepped out he muttered, "You look so worldly; it's disgraceful to me, please leave." He turned around and disappeared into the shop.

I stood in the driveway, speechless. It sounded like he had been rehearsing the exact words for the hundredth time. This was the third time I had come home to visit. The first two times had not gone well, but the letters he wrote to me after the second visit were polite and considerate. I thought he was finally ready to forgive me, but apparently it was all phony. I had driven 1258 miles to find out he still held a grudge and was not ready to accept me the way I was.

I looked at the house and saw some of the little ones standing at the kitchen door peeking out. *I wonder what all this is about; no one is coming out to greet me.* I grabbed the books and magazines I had brought to give to the kids and walked to the door. Tears welled up with my anger. To my surprise, Mem and Jacob were standing in the kitchen waiting for me to come in.

"What's wrong?" Jacob asked. "What did Datt have to say to you?"

"He told me to leave," I answered. "I just came in to drop off this box of books, and then I am getting out of here."

"Wait a minute," Jacob muttered. "I am going to have a talk with Datt. He is crazy for acting like this."

"Don't bother. If Datt doesn't want me to be here, then I would rather just leave and not cause a problem."

It was too late. Before I could even finish the sentence, Jacob bolted out the door, with Mem following behind. Jacob's reaction to all this surprised me. I was not sure how to take it, because the last time I came home to visit he did not have much to say. Something had changed.

They soon returned and told me it was okay for me to stay. Datt was just not in a good mood, but he had agreed to let me stay for a while.

Later that afternoon, Jacob and I sat on the porch with no one around. For the first time we had a long, deep discussion about our feelings. The brotherly conversation I had wanted so long ago was finally real, except now it was about a completely different subject.

I listened to Jacob talk in a soft voice for a while. I burst into tears when he said, "It has been so hard to move on since you left, and I can never fully accept your decision, but I do want you to be happy."

I cried softly. For the first time, I was not mad that Jacob told me exactly what was on his mind. It felt so good to have a conversation and not be yelled at or preached at like Datt always did.

When I could talk without blubbering like a baby, I said, "I feel very bad to put you and the rest of the family through so much pain, but there was no other choice. I was so unhappy and miserable the last few years that I just had leave. Going to the balloon doctor was just the last straw for me. During that treatment I decided to definitely get out of here. I was so angry with Datt for making me go there, I didn't know how to forgive him. I honestly believe that God has been watching over me and has given me the strength to go find a different life."

"Are you going to ever forgive Datt?" Jacob asked quietly.

I was silent for a second, then said, "Yes, I came here today to forgive him and I quickly found out he wasn't ready for it. I don't think I will ever forget, but forgiveness is the only way to live without pain from the past."

"Do you think you will come back to stay someday?" he asked, voice raspy, as if he was about to cry. He leaned over and braced his arms on his legs so I could not see his tears.

"At this point I don't see myself being Amish again," I said. "I wish I could come home so the family could be happy again. But I know that I wouldn't be happy, so why should I deprive myself and be miserable? The last thing I want to do is come back and then leave again if I can't make it here. I can't bear the thought of hurting the family twice."

"Well, I wish you would come back," he said in a hopeful tone. "But I see your point. It would be better if you wait until you are ready."

I did not say anything more. I sat in silence, wishing it would not be so difficult to explain why being Amish was not for me anymore. My heart ached. I wished there were words I could say that made sense. But my feelings were not explainable. It is kind of like the moment when a boyfriend suddenly breaks up with a girl with no specific explanation. The girl desperately wants closure to move on, but nothing the guy says helps the shattered heart, because there are no exact words that can make the hurt go away. At this point, the Good Man was the only One who could comfort Jacob and help him understand my feelings.

Soon Datt came out of the shop and sat behind me on a bench. He started talking about the good Lord and how evil the outside world had become. I let him talk without interrupting. Jacob sat silently as well. The preaching lasted for a good thirty minutes, and when Datt finally grew quiet I said as calmly as possible, "I appreciate your view, but everyone has their differences."

With that, I stood up and walked back into the house. I could not listen to one more word of Datt's preaching, and definitely did not want to start another argument. Datt did not talk to me the rest of my four-day visit, and I returned to Texas with a hole of sadness still open in my heart.

As I left the biology class an hour later, I could not believe I did not pay any attention to the teacher. All I remembered hearing was the teacher saying we would have an exam in a week. I was screwed.

§

A few days after zoning out in biology class, I stepped off a Southwest Airlines jet at the Kansas City airport. I was about to do something I swore I would never do. But after remembering how Jacob had rescued me from Datt's decision to make me leave, and because our conversation had been so fulfilling, I felt I needed to be at his wedding. It was such a big day for him and I wanted to show him my love and support. Besides, I knew the bride very well: we had gone to the same school, and she had been one grade ahead of me. She was our second cousin, and I was against marriage to such a close relative, but I had no control over it. After all, it happens all the time in the Amish community.

My parents' house was a two-hour drive from Kansas City, so Virgil and Jolene toted me from the airport to the house. I did not feel comfortable not having my own vehicle, in case I needed to make a run for it. However, I knew my parents did not want a car sitting on their property during the wedding, so I made an exception and hoped for the best. I had not talked to Datt since the last visit, but just like before he wrote me letters as if everything was normal. *I hope he does not pull that stunt on me again,* I prayed as I walked into the house.

Datt sat in his usual chair in the living room, pipe dangling from his mouth, visiting with several young men.

I walked over to him, greeted him with a handshake, and asked, *"Vee bisht du?"*

To my astonishment, he greeted me politely. I thought it was awkward to greet Datt with a handshake when he should have gotten out of his chair and given me a hug, but giving hugs was out of the question in my family.

Datt asked if I knew who the men were. They sat silently and stared at me as if they had never seen a girl wearing pants.

I looked at them for what seemed like a long minute. I had no idea who they were. Both of the guys had dark, thick beards and hair long enough to cover their ears and the back of their necks. They reminded me of gorillas. My face flushed from embarrassment.

Finally I said, "I am guessing you are my cousins, but I don't know your names." I offered them a handshake. Still they did not tell me their names. They were quieter than fence posts. Even more embarrassing, it looked like they were hurt because I did not know them.

Just when I thought I was not going to get an answer, Datt said, "They are your first cousins from Ohio."

After he told me their names, my heart stopped for a moment. I remembered playing with them many times when I lived in Ohio. I had seen them again when I was in my teens living in Missouri, but it was at least eight years since I had last seen them. I had almost three hundred first cousins and I did not know how I was supposed to remember them all. Since I had not been living with the Amish anymore, I noticed more than ever that the men's looks changed after they started growing beards, and eventually they all ended up looking the same.

"Really?" I said, surprised. "I am sorry I didn't recognize you, I would have never guessed."

One of them finally made an effort to say something, "I guess we all change in some ways."

I left the living room as politely as I could and went to the kitchen where the girls washed the supper dishes. I was relieved to finally see some familiar faces, and to be greeted happily. I waited until they finished the dishes, then we went upstairs to figure out what I was going to wear for the wedding. Mem joined us, sitting on the bed next to me. I had my cell phone in my hand and was trying to put it on vibrate, hoping she would not tell me to turn it off. I planned to hide it in a drawer close by, in case an emergency arose and I wanted to get away.

"I am concerned about your short hair," she said. "How are you going to put it in a bun to put under your head covering?"

"I don't know yet, but I will try and get it up somehow," I assured her.

"You shouldn't have cut your hair in the first place," she said, smiling a little.

"Ahh, I bought a wig that I was going to wear to make my hair longer. Would you like that better?" I joked.

She looked at me and quickly said, "No, I do not want you to wear a wig. I want you to be as real as possible for tomorrow."

Hmm… as real as possible. Did she think I was not real anymore? I brushed the comment aside. I was not about to tell Mem how I ended up with such short hair. The first haircut I had gotten after leaving the Amish fell just below my shoulders. The beautician had cut off twelve inches the first time, then coaxed me into keeping the locks as a souvenir even though I really wanted to be liberated of that long hair for good. One day I decided I wanted even shorter hair—it had been a dream of mine since I was young girl. I had told the beautician, Tiffany, I wanted my hair length to be right above my shoulders. Feeling a little giddy about the privilege of being able to cut my hair any way I wanted without fear of God punishing me, I sat smugly in the chair while Tiffany snipped away.

After a while Tiffany cheerfully said, "Look in the mirror to see the new you!"

As she swung my chair around and I came face-to-face with my reflection, my jaw dropped to my feet. I was mortified. I could not believe how much hair she had cut off; I thought she had scalped me! It was not the haircut I had envisioned. I looked like a boy! I lied to Tiffany and pretended I liked the haircut even though I was furious she had cut much more than I had wanted. I went home and cried my eyes out. *Dear God, you did not say in the Bible women cannot get boyish haircuts, did you?* I hoped not.

By wedding time, my hair had grown out enough to put it in a little ponytail. Mem would have been even more concerned to see me otherwise. The awkward silence soon broke when Sarah popped into the room with a dark red dress along with a nicely-pressed and folded cape, and an apron to go with the dress.

"Emma, this is my dress and I am so worried it won't fit you. Please try it on right now." She sounded like it was an emergency.

Everyone left the room to give me privacy while I changed. Sarah soon returned and looked at me with her twinkling blue eyes. The little smile on her face told me she was thinking something amusing about the way I looked.

"Why are you looking at me so funny?" I asked.

She laughed and said, "I am just glad you are here. I never thought you would actually come for the wedding, since you knew that you would be wearing Amish clothes."

"I am surprised at myself that I did come, but I wanted to be supportive for Jacob, and I knew you would want me to be here."

"Yeah, that is good. The only bad part is I won't get to visit with you because I will be *navahucking*."

"Oh shit! I never thought you would be the one. I knew Rhoda would be a *navahucka*, but not you too."

Suddenly I was devastated. *Navahucka* meant that she and Rhoda would be sitting next to the bride in the church service and following her wherever she went for the whole day. So would their boyfriends, except they would be sitting next to Jacob. They were considered the two maids of honor and the two best men.

After Sarah noticed the look on my face, she said in a serious voice, "I know it sucks, but I didn't have a choice."

We sat on the bed in silence for a little while. We both knew this would be our last conversation because I was leaving to go back to Texas early Friday morning, right after the wedding, and Sarah had to stay at the bride's house for the next two nights.

Finally Sarah said, "I best be getting ready to go. My boyfriend will be here soon to pick me up."

"Okay, go get ready and have fun tomorrow." I patted her back. She had written me a letter telling me about her boyfriend. At that moment, I realized she would never leave the Amish. My hopes for my sister to join me in the outside world had vanished for good.

As Sarah was leaving the room she stopped at the door and offered me some encouragement, "You will still have Amanda and Anna by your side tomorrow."

"Umm, yeah, I know. Don't worry about me, I will be just fine." Sarah's boyfriend, Abe, was the first guy I had a date with, and I did not want to revisit those memories, but there was no way of ignoring them. Abe was the bride's brother and an attractive guy, and by the look on Sarah's face I could tell she loved him. I just wished they were not so closely related.

Thank goodness I had plenty of sisters to get me through the next day. It was customary for the bridesmaids and their partners to spend the night before the wedding at the bride's house. There was no chance of me visiting with Sarah anymore because she would be drowning in a sea of people all day long. The only problem with Amanda and Anna was they had grown and changed so much in the last few years I felt like I did not know them anymore. Amanda was four years younger and about two inches taller than me. She looked a lot like me, but just did not think like me. Amanda was more serious with the Amish life and was content with the way things were. Sweet little Anna had grown into a younger version of Sarah: funny, blonde, blue-eyed, and full of energy, ready to play jokes whenever possible.

That night I went to bed early because I felt sick. I had a bad migraine headache and heartburn like nobody's business. I knew it was all just nerves from worrying about who I would have to face the next day. It had already gotten off to a bad start downstairs when I did not know who my cousins were, and I could only imagine what tomorrow would be like.

The next thing I knew, Mem was standing at the bottom of the stairs calling my brother Noah's name, telling him it was time to get up. I waited to see if she would call my name too, like she used to when I was living at home. I heard the door close and the footsteps fall silently away. *No, she was not going to call my name, maybe it was just too hard for her to say my name again after so many years of not being here.* However, she had told me the night before that I needed to get up at five o'clock and be ready to go with Noah to the wedding by six o'clock. The rest of the family planned to leave later. Mem wanted me to go early so I could see Jacob before too many people arrived. Jacob was at his in-laws' house. It took almost an hour to get there by horse and buggy.

I rolled out of bed and it took me a second to realize there was no light switch to turn on. *It would be so much easier to flip on a light switch*, I grumbled as I felt around the nightstand for matches to light the oil lamp. It was so dark I could not even see my hand when I held it up close to my face. Finally I got the lamp lit and the light it cast was barely better than no light at all. I did not know how we survived with just a small flame for light. I put on the dress Sarah gave me the night before. I was pinning on the cape when Mem knocked on the door and walked in.

"Do you still know how to put a cape on?" she asked.

"I guess so, I haven't poked myself yet with these straight pins, I think it's because I still know how," I said. In a more serious voice I said, "I am more concerned with how I look."

"Let me help you get these pleats right on your back. I don't want your cape too far out on your shoulders." She offered to help me.

153

With cold hands, she stuck the ends of the cape between the dress collar and my neck, making three pleats down the full length of my back.

"It would help if I had big mirror so can see what I am doing," I said. "My hands are sweating from trying to put this pin in the back."

"What's wrong with the little hand mirror laying right there?" She pointed to the nightstand.

"I can't see with it, it's too little, and the light in this room does not help," I muttered.

As soon as those words left my mouth I wished I could take them back. I did not want to complain while I was here, especially not in front of Mem. She did not say anything about my comment, but I could tell she did not want to bring up the fact there was nothing she could do about it. Rules dictated the Amish could not have big mirrors, and having a dim light in the house was like bright sunshine to them. Years ago, using a dim oil lamp did not bother me, but now I was used to having a light blaring in every corner of my apartment, whether it was dark outside or not.

I was glad when Mem changed the subject and said, "I need to go downstairs again, to finish making breakfast, but first I want to help you get your head covering on to make sure it fits right."

I sat down on the bed and started the process of putting my short hair up. Even though my hair had grown out since my last haircut, it was still way shorter than Amish are used to seeing. I used one of Sarah's handmade hair bands to pull back every strand away from my face. I managed to keep my hair up with several hairpins. Then I put on the white pleated covering Mem had ironed and prepared yesterday.

I held the mirror up to my face and gasped: I looked exactly like I did a long time ago. My throat went dry and my heart leaped out of my chest. I was Amish again and I did not like it. The look on Mem's face told me she enjoyed it. I wanted to say, *Just don't get your hopes up that I will stay like this,* but I did not want to ruin the sweet mother time we were enjoying. It did not happen too often, and I longed to have a close relationship with her. Back in Texas, I would get green with envy when other girls went out with their mothers on special mother-daughter dates.

When I glanced backed to Mem, she was smiling from ear to ear, "Ya, it fits. You might have to pull it forward every once-in-a-while; it seems to pull back a little. And I hope your hair stays up all day, so you don't have to fix it again. I don't want other people to see that you cut your hair."

"I will do my best to keep my hair covered, Mem," I said, trying to sound reassuring so she would not worry about me all day.

"Okay, come downstairs to eat soon. It is almost time for you to leave for the wedding," she said with a serious look on her face.

I was already fidgeting in my dress and I had only been in it for less than an hour. The collar squeezed my neck tightly, but it had to be tight so the cape would stay in place. I was glad I decided to wear a bra; at least something felt familiar. I was afraid Mem would notice I had one on when she helped me with the cape. She probably would not know what it was since women here did not wear them. After I finished griping to myself, I ran downstairs to eat and, out of all things that could possibly be made for breakfast, it had to be coffee soup. I should have known because it was an Amish breakfast classic, made with hot milk, sugar, and coffee, and eaten with bread or Saltine crackers. Not my favorite meal at all.

While I ate, I thought about all the food I could eat back in Texas, and it did not include coffee soup. I loved having a microwave oven where food could be cooked in seconds, or where food could also explode in seconds. I soon learned that mistake when I tried to cook an egg in one, and it exploded with such force the egg shredded to fine pieces. Microwavable food is not nearly as healthy as Amish-cooked meals, but I was glad to be spending more time on things I wanted to do, and spending less time cooking meals for an army. I was selfish.

Chapter 9:

The Past is Always the Past

Don't go where the path may lead, go instead where there is no path.

~ Ralph Emerson ~

The morning of Jacob's wedding dawned cloudy, and the chilly September air nipped at my cheeks as I rode in the buggy with my brother Noah to the house where Jacob was to be married. Daylight began to break, but the gray clouds hung low in the sky, looking sad. The sun did not even bother to peek out from behind the clouds and the rolling hills. I hoped it would not rain because that would be a bad sign for Jacob's wife-to-be. It had been such a long time since I sat on a buggy behind a horse; I had forgotten how bad it smelled. It was obvious no one had brushed the horse that morning because loose dust and hair fell from its coat and blew into my face. The horse farted. When I was Amish, I took things like horse farts as part of normal life, but now it bothered me. It would not have been so bad if I had not been sitting right behind the horse's rear end, but my seat made it impossible to escape the animal's stench; apparently I had become a city girl over the last two-and-a-half years. Driving a motorized vehicle was much more satisfying, and it did not stink like horse farts.

We arrived at the house a little before seven o'clock. Noah dropped me off by the sidewalk leading to the front door. I dreaded opening the door and facing reality, but since I was one of the first ones to arrive, I thought maybe it might not be so bad. My sister, Amanda, had stayed overnight at the wedding house to help with last-minute chores, so I did not get to see her at my parents' the night before. She was washing breakfast dishes when I walked in and she welcomed me with a smile. "Where should I put my bonnet and shawl?" I asked her.

Amanda warmly replied, "Take it upstairs to the room on the right."

I was glad to have a reason to go upstairs because I knew Sarah was there dressing for the day.

I put up my shawl and bonnet and walked to the next room down the hall. Anxious and excited wedding folks filled the room, trying to get dressed. They greeted me when I walked in. Jacob was tying his shiny black shoes, and his wife-to-be frantically tried to pin her cape. By Amish tradition, the bride and groom were allowed see each other the day of the wedding. They usually would spend the wedding night together in the same house, usually at the bride's parents'.

Jacob shook my hand after he finished tying his shoes. "I am glad you could make it today," he said quietly. "I didn't really expect you to come."

"I am happy to be here on your special day," I replied, even though half of me did not really want to be there. *Now I better try to act like I am happy, not just say it*, I thought.

Sarah, Rhoda, and Anna wore their dark blue dresses with white aprons and capes. Dark blue was the standard color for the bride and bridesmaids. The girls had to take turns using a small mirror to see how their dresses fit. The girls complained continuously about the way they looked. *Oh, this cape doesn't fit right, help me with the pin in the back, I can't get the pleat right, it's hot in here, my hair needs to be fixed again, how do I look now? Blah, blah, blah.* It made my complaining earlier that morning seem minor compared to what I heard from them. My head spun listening to them, and seeing the guys I had once dated gathered in the same room made it seem much worse.

Abe was there, as handsome as ever. His dark blue fitted suit, brown straight hair, blue eyes, and a smile to kill for, made him look extra sleek this morning. Sarah was lucky to have him for a boyfriend, and maybe— eventually—a husband. He was five years older than she was, old enough to be married, but he had taken his time and waited for the right girl. I could not help but wonder if he remembered that awful first date with me. I mentally kicked myself in the butt and thought, *of course he remembers.* It was something that just would not go away no matter how hard I tried to erase it.

Rhoda's boyfriend, Enos, was a complete stranger to me. He was a young man from Ohio and they were in a long-distance relationship. They had started dating after I left home, and for all I knew he was also a second cousin. He looked handsome as well. He did not say much while I was in the room, but he stared at me all day long. He probably could not imagine having a future sister-in-law living out in the free world.

I stood against the wall and observed everything going on. I could not help wondering where I would fit in to all of this activity if I were still Amish. I would probably be a *navahucka* instead of Sarah, but who would be my partner? Would that partner also be the one I would marry? I looked at Norman, my ex-boyfriend who had just walked into the room a few minutes earlier. He laughed and talked more than the others, and sometimes I caught a glimpse of him looking at me. I had left the Amish a couple months after I broke up with him. After the break up, I wondered if I had made the right decision; he looked better now than when I dated him. He had grown into a handsome and charming young man. *No,* I thought, *I would not want Norman to be my boyfriend.* I could not see myself marrying him or any other Amish guy. As much as I tried, I could not picture myself being anywhere but back in Texas and in college.

After everyone finished dressing, they all stomped downstairs and climbed into a buggy waiting outside to take them to the neighbor's house where the wedding service itself was to be held. I stayed behind and helped set the tables with endless lines of china dishes, and I prepared to be a table waiter for hundreds of people. It was tradition that the nearest neighbor held the wedding church service at their house, so the bride's house had enough room to prepare the big lunch and dinner after the wedding. The wedding service usually started at 8:00 and lasted until about 12:30. It was similar to a regular Amish church service, except it lasted an hour longer, and at twelve o'clock the couple exchanged marriage vows. At the bride's house, the women, usually the bride's aunts or neighbors, prepared an amazing lunch which would be ready by the time the service finished.

After the bride and groom left the house for the wedding, the morning got livelier as women and girls began to arrive. The women came to cook while the girls helped setting and waiting on tables. Some of the girls still remembered me from when I was Amish, but instead of acknowledging me, they walked away with shocked looks on their faces. I was astonished. Why wouldn't they say something to me? The girls who did not know me would sit right next to me. They did not know the difference. But when Cousin Lizzie walked into the room she stopped short and gasped. With eyes wide open, she grabbed the two nearest girls and dragged them into the hallway. When they returned, their sheepish looks confirmed Lizzie had told them who I was. I could just imagine Lizzie telling her friends I was the girl who went "high," and was now destined for hell. One-by-one, they stared at me, and the whispering began. I sat on a chair and pretended not to notice, but their reaction disgusted me. I told myself over-and-over, *I came here for my brother, not for the judgmental hypocrites.*

Finally, at nine o'clock, it was time to start preparing the big feast. We all went downstairs where the married women busily peeled potatoes. Since I was a table waiter, along with all the other girls, I had to start setting the tables with the finest china dishes. I worked in the living room, busily laying sticks of butter on little plates, when I caught a glimpse of Aunt Mary standing at the doorway. Mary was married to Datt's brother, Joe. When she saw me she covered her mouth, spun around, and ran back into the kitchen. I went to the doorway and peeked around the corner to see what she would do next. I spied her whispering to other local women. *Huh, how childish*, I thought. She did the same thing her daughter Lizzie had just done. Soon I heard my name spreading around like the flu in an Amish house; it did not look like many women were happy I was there. Maybe they thought I was a threat to their daughters.

While I stood at the doorway watching the women's reaction, I caught a glimpse of Mem standing at the kitchen sink, talking to someone with her back turned. I could not see who it was. I wondered how she would take it if she knew what went on behind her back. Or did she already know? I thought maybe people were giving her a hard time, too, because I was her daughter. I felt sorry for her. I scurried back to my place before anyone noticed, and continued filling butter dishes. Every now and then, I caught one or two women peeking into the living room as if they had to see for themselves that I was actually at the wedding being a bad influence on their daughters.

I was glad when the time came to go to the basement to cut cakes, slice cheese, and whip cream for the puddings and tapioca. In the basement, I stayed a little more hidden from all the women upstairs. I felt more at ease when my sister, Amanda, stood beside me to peel apples for the fruit salad. We talked for a while, and soon some of Amanda's friends started to open up and ask me questions as they gathered around me.

"What are you doing in Texas?" someone asked.

"I am just going to college right now," I replied.

I realized by their stunned faces they did not know what college was, and I think it scared them. They went back to talking about usual Amish life, which was okay with me. At least they were talking to me about things that were comfortable for them.

By 11:30 we finished up in the basement, and all the table waiters sat down to eat the great meal before it was time to feed the others. I was hungry and exhausted, but there was no time to chew the food, just swallow and take the next bite. I could not believe how fast everyone ate. I was relieved I had not been baptized in the Amish church before I left home because I would have been forced to eat at a table by myself as part of the shunning process. When someone does something that is not in the *Ordnung*, which is the basic outline of written rules dictating almost every aspect of Amish life, church ministers may attempt to intervene in the conflict and try to solve the issue. However, to return to good standing, shunned members must show submission even if they believe they are innocent. Only when there is a complete break from the community does the excommunication become permanent. Since I left the Amish, I made an effort to understand shunning, and what I came up with is pretty simple: Shunning works a little bit like an electric fence around a pasture with a pretty good fence charger on it. It is the most important fallback the church uses to make people feel guilty for their actions.

I believe love casts out all fear and evil doings. If the Amish could understand the love God has for us all, they could engage in a way that would draw them closer to Him, not push them away. This would eliminate the shunning and bring repentance to the person instead of shame. Shunning them for a while does not mean they will ever repent, since it is driven by fear rather than by love.

After we finished eating, it was time to go to the wedding service and watch the exchanging of the marriage vows. We piled into several buggies and drove ten-minutes to the service. The cooks stayed behind to finish last-minute cooking details.

At the service, my Datt helped the girls find a place in the crowded house to sit. There were so many people there I could not even move my legs where I sat without hitting someone else. People looked at me like they thought I was from another planet. Essentially, I was from another planet, but a better one. I guessed they did not see too many runaways who came back home and dressed Amish for a wedding.

I tried not focus too much on the people staring at me because there were too many other distractions. Uncle Moses, my mem's brother and an ordained bishop from Ohio, stood at the living room doorway and preached. He had performed a lot of weddings and baptisms in his life, and he made that quite obvious by preaching faster and better than anyone I had ever heard. But I still had no clue now what he said, just like I never understood any church services growing up. I was glad I was not getting married in a place where I would have to sit still for more than four hours before I could say "I do" while having no clue what the preacher was saying. To me it was like playing house, just going through the motions without having any meaning. Now that I was back with the Amish for a day, I was completely convinced I could never be happy if I decided to come back for good. It just did not feel right. I was not comfortable. I did not feel pretty, and I felt like I was powerless.

Before I could think too much about the Amish church, the bishop called Jacob and Anna to stand next to him. They had been dating for at least three years and seemed to be a match made in heaven. Anna was tall, with blue eyes and dirty blonde hair, and her laughter resonated with happiness. After the groom and bride made their way to the bishop, everyone stood for the reading of the scriptures. The bride and groom faced the bishop instead of each other when they said their "I do's." Jacob bowed his head, face flushed. I thought he looked happy, but I could not really read his expression. Anna smiled slightly, stood as straight as a wall, and kept her eyes glued on the bishop. She looked pretty in her dark blue dress and white cape. After they exchanged vows, they went back to their seats. The vows were in a different language than the German spoken outside of church. I assumed the vows were similar to those spoken during an English wedding, but there was no "you may kiss the bride" moment. I had never seen an Amish couple kiss in public, and I was not quite sure I wanted to see it either.

After the bishop pronounced the couple married, the entire group of table waiters stood up at once and hurried back to the kitchen to get ready for the rush of the big crowd.

I was honored to be a table waiter in the same room where Jacob and Anna sat. Traditionally the bride and groom sat in a corner called the *eck*. It was a special place where every newlywed couple sat and was served before anyone else. Rhoda and Enos sat on the Jacob's side. Sarah and Abe sat on Anna's side. After the bride and groom took their seats, the rest of the table in the living room filled with fifty or more married men and young single men. The wives and girls ate at a big table in the basement and kitchen. Some of the tables had to be filled twice to feed everyone.

After everyone took their seats, they all bowed their heads, the bishop said silent prayer, and the rush of eating began. Being a table waiter was so out of place for me, I was sure I would drop something. I carried bowls of mashed potatoes, gravy, dressing, salads, big plates of fried chicken, and cheese slices. For dessert, we served peaches, two kinds of cakes—a white walnut cake and a chocolate cake—and blueberry and pecan pies. The men gulped the food down as if they had not eaten anything for a week.

It was loud: everyone talked and laughed, celebrating the joy of two people getting married. Some of the men even wanted to talk to me; they were not nearly as critical and judgmental as the women were. I began to relax, and I talked to as many people as I could. I was glad I could still speak German very well. It proved I had not yet abandoned all of my Amish blood.

Jacob and Anna looked radiant as they visited with the people surrounding them. During that moment, I was happy I had come back to celebrate with them, even if it meant being looked down upon. I wished I could have taken pictures of them, but in their minds, they did not need pictures to remember this special day. It would be forever ingrained into their memories. I stared at Jacob. His dark brown hair was perfectly cut for an Amish man. He had started to grow a beard, but it was not visible unless I looked closely. I wondered if his beard was going to grow out thick and long like most other men. I hoped not. For the first time I realized I really loved my brother. If only I could tell him, but I knew it would embarrass him.

§

The moment everyone finished eating, the women stacked piles and piles of dishes together to be washed and dried with towels. It seemed like an endless job, and I began to feel worn out from the stress of being around so many people. It was late in the afternoon before we finally finished washing the dishes, and only then could we take a short break before it was time to start cooking supper.

After we cleaned up the living room, the men gathered to sing hymns. Jacob and his two best men stood outside and handed out cigars to the men, while Anna and her maids of honor handed out candy bars to the women and children. I went upstairs thinking I could find a place to relax a little bit, but no such luck: it was so crowded it made my head swim. All at once I was ready to get out of this noisy place. I realized I did not belong there anymore. I began to panic and thought this place was just way too Amish for me. Fear of getting stuck and not being able to leave crept over me.

I searched the house for my mem but could not find her. I felt like a lost little girl. Suddenly she appeared out of nowhere and asked me how I was doing.

"I want to leave and go back home," I said. "This place is getting to be too much for me, I've had enough for today."

"Well, it's almost time for Noah to go home and do the chores; you can maybe go with him," she said calmly.

About that time, Datt showed up too. "I am sending Noah home to do chores in a little bit. Are any of the girls going too?" he asked Mem.

"Yes, I want to go," I piped up.

He looked surprised. "Are you coming back again for supper?" I shook my head. "You don't want to be here till midnight then?" I could hear the sadness in his voice. Maybe he was sad because he thought I would suddenly be overcome by some young man and would want to stay Amish so I could marry him. I felt like I was letting Datt down.

"No, I don't want to stay that long," I answered quietly. "And I especially don't want to go down to the basement with all the young guys and girls." I did not want anyone else to hear me.

Usually after supper was over, all the young unmarried folks old enough to date would go down to the basement to chat and play games. Then, at midnight, the single guys and girls would pair up and march upstairs in a single file with the dating couples to sit around the living room table and sing songs. It was a big deal for the married people to see who was sitting with whom at the table. *What if no guy wanted to be my partner?* I thought. I decided I did not want that embarrassment, so I pressed the point of wanting to go home. Besides, my used-to-be friends were not talking to me, so I decided I did not need to be there to be the butt of their silly game.

"I don't blame her," Mem chimed in after an awkward silence. "But you will be at home by yourself because Noah is coming back after he is done with the chores, and we are all staying till midnight."

"That will be fine with me," I answered. "I am so tired I will be going to bed early and will be asleep anyway."

Datt said, "If you are sure about going home, then go get your bonnet and shawl. I am going out to the barn to let Noah know you are going with him."

I was so relieved Datt was being a good sport and did not try to talk me into staying. This was the first visit home that Datt did not start an argument with me. The ride home was much more pleasant than the morning ride to the wedding. After Noah finished the chores, I gave him two bags of candy I had in my suitcase. He stuffed a few handfuls into his pocket, and he was delighted I had brought candy all the way from Texas. After stuffing his pockets, Noah drove back to the wedding place.

I was now all alone in my parents' house, just what I needed. I went to the room that used to be mine before I left home and lay on the bed. It brought back so many memories I started to cry. I realized I missed my family more than I could have ever imagined, but my life was different now and I would not surrender. My heart and soul longed for my parents' love and acceptance, but I was not born to remain Amish, and I knew the Good Man had plans for me in the outside world.

Finally, after an hour of reminiscing, I got up from the bed, took off my long, uncomfortable dress, and put on my own comfy night pajamas. I was so ready to hit the bed, even though it felt like a sack of rocks. I felt relieved knowing that when I woke up again I would be heading back to Texas where I belonged. I did not care that living independently was hard work and a huge responsibility. Even though I was homesick for my family, I knew I could not have the best of both worlds. My new world, though far from perfect, suited me just fine.

§

I made it back to Texas just in time for me to give a speech in one of my animal science classes. The subject was about diseases in pigs, which I had no clue about, but I had prepared a Power Point presentation nonetheless. I thought I was capable of winging my way through it. Boy, was I wrong! I got up in front of the class and went blank. For the life of me, I could not get my stubborn tongue to speak. I almost burst into tears. I was still stressed and emotional from my days in Amish land; no one in the classroom knew

I had just flown back home for my brother's wedding. They did not know I had become Amish again for a few days and had returned to my English life in hopes of giving a speech about pig diseases. Living two lives was wearisome. My teacher saved me from complete failure by asking questions about the information I had found from the research. Afterwards, I went home and slept for thirteen hours straight.

I made it through each semester without any more embarrassing brain freezes. In December of 2009, almost three years after leaving the Amish, I graduated with an Associate's degree in Agriculture Technology from Texas State Technical College in Harlingen, Texas, and without missing a semester, I transferred to Tarleton State University in Stephenville, Texas, to get my Bachelor's degree in Science. I moved eight hours away from the few friends I had, to find myself all alone again. I did not know a single soul at Tarleton, but with gratitude, I kept my head up and continued making paths where there was none. Of course, I could not help but wish my Mem and Datt would have shown an interest in my happiness, but I know the Good Man is.

A list of answers to the most frequently-asked questions

No question is a stupid question...

Are you still considered Amish?
No, I sometimes refer to myself as ex-Amish when people ask why I talk with an accent.

Could someone not Amish join an Amish community?
Yes, people have done it. However, I would not advise anyone to do so, because of the rules imposed by the Amish. If you grow up Amish, at least you have an understanding of them, but an Englisher trying to come in would most likely develop an argumentative attitude toward those rules. If someone has a personality in which being a follower comes naturally, it can be done. You just have to be sure of why you are doing it, and then abandon all other "why" questions after you join. Asking questions as to why something has to be done "this way" instead of "that way" will get you nowhere.

Which gender is easier to join the Amish, man or woman?
I would say it is harder for women than men. For one thing, women have to "submit" to a lot more than men do, including deferring to the husband's authority. Of course,

this also depends on the nature of the person joining, but one basically cannot be resistant to "submission" to the Amish religion and way-of-life and still be accepted into the Amish community.

What is the one thing you love the most now?
Any drive-thru eating place. I think it is just too cool to drive up to a window and pick up food. Healthy or not.

How was it being Amish?
I have told many people, it's kind of like getting two feet of snow: it looks very pretty when you are in your warm house looking out at it, but if you really need to go out in it, it's not so pretty any more. It's different for everyone. Those who are content with being Amish will not have any problems with accepting the rules.

Why did your Amish group not practice *rumspringa* ?
I don't know except I would think it is not allowed because it leads to too many temptations. Besides, *rumspringa* is blown way out of proportion in the general public. It's not nearly as common a practice as many people claim.

What are the names of all your brothers and sisters?
Jacob, (me), Rhoda, Samuel, Sarah, Amanda, Noah, Anna, Dennis, Mary, Esther, Lizzie, Fannie, and Levi. Dad's name is Jonas, and Mom's name is Katie.

What does the initial 'J' stand for in your middle name?
Every Amish family has the tradition of giving their children just an initial for a middle name. The initial comes from the first letter of the father's name, Jonas. Middle

names are not allowed in the Swartzentruber community. All my siblings have a J for their middle name.

What does a typical Amish bathroom look like?
The bathroom (outhouse) is usually built behind the house, and since it cannot be flushed like a toilet in a modern bathroom, it is washed down with water from the garden hose every once-in-a-while. Some of them are not even modern enough to have a hose to wash it out with, so they shovel it out instead. Also, a typical outhouse usually has enough room for two adults and a younger child at the same time. Sometimes, in my family, four or five girls would use the outhouse at once.

Why were you born in a hospital when it wasn't common for Amish to do that?
I assume my mother was having complications with me, however, I never asked her why I wasn't born at home. Talking about childbirth never happened in our house. Ever.

Is it easier to cook meals now than it was at home with a wood stove?
Yes, much easier! I can cook a full meal in 30 minutes on an electric stove versus several hours on a wood stove.

Are perfumes or scented lotions allowed?
In my community, perfumes and scented lotions were not allowed. We couldn't wear anything that would draw attention to us. The same goes with jewelry and rings. However, girls could wear rings made out of pennies.

When you were in the Amish, were you aware of the fascination the "English" have with the Amish?

I was never aware of the fascination the "English" have for the Amish while I was living in the community. However, it did feel like we were a phenomenon, in many ways, but the funny thing is, I did not enjoy the attention from the "English" because I was embarrassed by the way I looked, or especially by my inability to understand and speak English very well when required. I absolutely hated those who made fun of us, and that was more often than you'd think. Since I left the Amish, I have realized how many people are fascinated by that lifestyle, but having lived it for eighteen years, I just don't get it.

About the Author

Emma Gingerich left her Amish community in Eagleville, Missouri, at the age of eighteen. She went to south Texas, close to South Padre Island, where she lived for almost four years. She received her Associates Degree at a community college and transferred to Tarleton State University located in Stephenville, Texas, to complete her Bachelor's Degree. She is currently pursuing her Master's Degree in business administration. Though Emma works full-time as a Billing Coordinator in the healthcare industry and is continuing her college education, she still managed to write her first memoir. She is looking forward to writing a sequel.

Education is important to Emma, and she is happy to have the opportunity to attend college. She hopes to help and inspire other Ex-Amish people to receive an education as well. Her passions are: writing, hiking, traveling, running and helping others.